Rethinking Federalism

Block Grants and Federal, State, and Local Responsibilities

Claude E. Barfield

D1522859

American Enterprise Institute for Public Policy Research
Washington and London

99318

Claude E. Barfield, a visiting fellow at the American Enterprise Institute, served from 1979 to 1981 as co–staff director of the President's Commission for a National Agenda for the Eighties.

Library of Congress Cataloging in Publication Data

Barfield, Claude E.
    Rethinking federalism.

.   (AEI studies ; 349)
    1. Block grants—United States.   2. Intergovernmental
fiscal relations—United States.   3. Federal government—
United States.   I. Title.   II. Series.
HJ275.B29   336.1'85   81–17602
ISBN 0–8447–3479–9   AACR2

AEI Studies 349

Printed in the United States of America

Contents

Preface

This monograph started with one object and ended with another. The initial purpose was to analyze the workings of block grants and to explore the likely administrative and political results of the Reagan administration's proposals to consolidate almost 100 existing categorical grant-in-aid programs into 6 large-scale grants to states. Very quickly it became apparent, however, that the president's long-range goals go beyond mere changes in the forms of grants; they raise important and profound questions regarding the nature and function of American federalism in the 1980s. Thus, what evolved finally from the analysis was a suggested framework for reordering federal, state, and local responsibilities. Under the proposal recommended in this study, the national government would move over the next few years to complete the national social agenda by assuming policy and financial responsibility for welfare reform and national health insurance. In turn, it would hand over to state and local governments a number of its current functions and programs in other areas such as education, transportation, community and economic development, social services, law enforcement, health, and environment—just to name some of the leading candidates for devolution.

Chapters 1–5 encompass the initial purpose of the study: to analyze the six block-grant proposals in the context of the history and current functioning of the federal grant system. Chapter 1 describes the current intergovernmental grant system and the theories which have been advanced over the years to provide a basis for that system. Chapter 2 traces the programmatic history of the federal grant system, emphasizing the political sinews that have developed over the years. Chapter 3 presents the Reagan administration's initial plans regarding block grants and federalism. Chapter 4 analyzes the working of five existing block grants and lays out a set of model provisions to be included in legislative proposals regarding block grants. Chapter 5 discusses the political consequences that may result from a substantial movement from categorical grants to block grants.

Finally, chapter 6 presents the rationale for a reshuffling of federal, state, and local responsibilities along the lines described above.

It sets forth both the political and the substantive cases for the federal government's taking over policy direction and financing for welfare and health care, while transferring to state and local governments many programs that would be more effectively administered and financed subnationally.

·   ·   ·

The initial draft of this book was completed before Congress finished action on the administration's block-grant proposals, and the material relating to final congressional determinations was inserted just as the study was going to press. Compared with the president's spectacular congressional victories on budgetary and tax policy, the new federalism proposals relating to block grants fared much less well. Congress made substantial changes in both the form and the substance of the administration's legislative recommendations, adding a number of restrictions and refusing to include some of the most sizable and important categorical aid programs.

The issues relating to block grants and to a sorting out of federal, state, and local responsibilities will remain current. The president vowed to state and local officials that he will continue to press Congress to remove the restrictions placed upon the existing block grants and to expand the number of categorical programs included in these block grants. In addition, the administration announced plans to bring forward new block grant proposals in January, 1982.

On July 30, 1981, just after his sweeping victory in the House of Representatives on the tax bill, President Reagan told the National Conference of State Legislatures:

> This nation has never fully debated the fact that over the past forty years federalism—one of the most essential and underlying principles of our Constitution—has nearly disappeared as a guiding force in American politics and government. My administration intends to initiate such a debate. . . .
>
> In normal times, what we've managed to get through the Congress concerning block grants would be a victory. Yet we did not provide the states with the degree of freedom in dealing with the budget cuts we had ardently hoped for. We got some categorical grants incorporated into block grants, but many of our block grant proposals are still on the Hill. That doesn't mean the end of the dream. Together you and I will be going back and back and back until we obtain the flexibility you need and deserve. The ultimate objective as I have told some of you is to use block grants as a bridge leading to the day when you will have not only the re-

sponsibility for programs that properly belong at the state level but you'll have the tax resources now usurped by Washington returned to you—ending that round trip of the people's money to Washington and back minus a carrying charge.

1

The Federal Grant System

There are basically three kinds of federal grants to state and local governments: categorical grants, block grants, and general revenue-sharing funds. In differentiating between the three types of grants, the Advisory Commission on Intergovernmental Relations (ACIR) has proposed three criteria:

- the range of federal administrators' funding discretion
- the range of recipient discretion concerning aided activities
- the type, number, detail, and scope of grant program conditions

The system is best envisioned as a continuum or spectrum, extending from maximum federal controls (generally associated with categorical grants) to maximum recipient discretion (generally associated with revenue sharing).

Categorical grants, in most cases, can be used only for specific, narrowly defined purposes. There are four types of categorical grants: formula grants, project grants, formula-project grants, and open-end reimbursement grants. Under the terms of a formula grant, funds are allocated according to factors enumerated in the authorizing legislation. For project grants, potential recipients submit individual applications to federal administrators who award grants on the basis of statutory guidelines. Formula-project grants combine a statutory formula with project applications and discretionary awards. Finally, for open-end reimbursement grants, the federal government reimburses state and local governments for a fixed proportion of their program costs. Among the four types of categorical programs, project grants generally place the most restraints on recipients because federal administrators use their discretionary power to impose precise performance conditions and to circumscribe narrowly the choice of permitted activities.

At the opposite end of the spectrum is general revenue sharing in which money is distributed to state and local governments by formula, with few limits on the purposes for which it may be spent and few procedural restrictions.

1

Block grants constitute a middle ground between categorical grants and general revenue sharing. Block grants are commonly defined as programs "in which funds are provided chiefly to general purpose governmental units in accordance with a statutory formula for use in a broad functional area largely at the recipient's discretion."[1]

More specifically, the ACIR has posited five design characteristics of block grants:

1. Federal aid is authorized for a wide range of activities within a broadly defined functional area.

2. Recipients have substantial discretion in identifying problems and designing programs and allocating resources to deal with those problems.

3. Administrative rules, fiscal reporting, planning, and other federally imposed requirements are kept to the minimum amount necessary to ensure that national goals are being accomplished.

4. Federal aid is distributed on the basis of a statutory formula, which results in narrowing federal administrators' discretion and providing a sense of fiscal certainty to recipients.

5. Eligibility provisions are specified by statute; general-purpose governmental units are favored as recipients, and elected officials and administrative generalists are favored as decisionmakers.

There exist today five block-grant programs which fulfill the design characteristics described above. They are the Partnership in Health Act of 1966 (health), the Omnibus Crime Control and Safe Streets Act of 1968 (law enforcement), the Comprehensive Employment and Training Act of 1973 (manpower training), the Housing and Community Development Act of 1974 (community development), and the Title XX Amendments of 1975 to the Social Security Act (social services).

In his study *The New Federalism*, political scientist Michael D. Reagan explained the administrative and political reasoning behind the move toward block grants:

> Just as the grant system as a whole stands somewhere between total state-local autonomy and total federal takeover of specific functions, so also does the block grant constitute

[1] For the definition of elements of the federal government grant-in-aid system, see Advisory Commission on Intergovernmental Relations (hereinafter ACIR), *Categorical Grants: Their Role and Design* (Washington, D.C., 1978), pp. 5–9; ACIR, *Block Grants: A Comparative Analysis* (Washington, D.C., 1977), p. 6; Carl W. Stenberg, "Block Grants: The Middlemen of the Federal Aid System," *Intergovernmental Perspective* (Spring 1977), pp. 8–13; Timothy J. Conlan, "Back in Vogue: The Politics of Block Grant Legislation," *Intergovernmental Perspective* (Spring 1981), pp. 8–17.

(at least potentially) a reasonable compromise between the values of categorical grants and shared revenues. Federal *policy* is very clearly stated in the laws authorizing the block grant programs, and if there is adequate means for ensuring programmatic accountability of the recipient governments, then such grants may be a useful way of centralizing policy while decentralizing administration and permitting considerable local choice and decisionmaking on particular programs.[2]

Because of the particular characteristics of the consolidation proposals which have been advanced by the Reagan administration, one other grant subcategory should be noted: the special revenue-sharing grants of the Nixon administration. In 1971, President Nixon proposed a series of special revenue-sharing bills that would have combined 129 categorical programs into six separate grants. The proposals were similar to earlier block-grant proposals in that they covered broad functional areas, narrowly defined eligible recipients, and distributed most of the funds as entitlements. The special revenue-sharing bills, however, contained far fewer strings than existing or later block grants: for instance, there were no matching requirements, little provision was made for federal auditing or oversight, and funds were to be paid automatically to the states and localities, without prior federal approval of plans for their use.[3] In their specific provisions, the Reagan proposals more nearly resemble the Nixon special revenue-sharing bills than they do existing block grants.

While the above definitions and characteristics of federal grant programs are both useful and broadly accurate, two points of caution should be noted. First, in actual practice there is a good deal of blurring and overlapping of the distinctions among grant types. Second, over time most of the programs have been amended and revised substantially, thus further complicating definitional rigor. Illustrative of the first point is the history of Title I of the Elementary and Secondary Education Act of 1965, a large formula-based categorical program, which for much of its history has operated like a block grant. Illustrative of the second point are the histories of several block grants which reflect a tendency for Congress to add restrictions that in effect "recategorize" these programs. For instance, forty-five new requirements were added to the Omnibus Crime Control and

---

[2] Michael D. Reagan, *The New Federalism* (New York: Oxford University Press, 1972), p. 63.

[3] ACIR, *Special Revenue Sharing: An Analysis of the Administration's Grant Consolidation Proposals* (Washington, D.C., 1971), pp. 8–18; George F. Break, *Financing Government in a Federal System* (Washington, D.C.: Brookings Institution, 1980), pp. 168–79.

Safe Streets Act during the eight years following its enactment. In the health area, instead of expanding the jurisdiction of the Partnership in Health block grant, Congress, between 1966 and 1980, surrounded it with twenty new categorical programs in the same functional area.[4]

Federal Allocation by Grant Form

Until the mid-1960s, categorical program aid formed a virtual monopoly in the intergovernmental grant system. The first block grant, the comprehensive health grant, was not established until 1966; and general revenue sharing did not come along until 1972. In fiscal 1972, the year before general revenue sharing was passed, categorical programs constituted 97 percent of all federal grants-in-aid; broad-based grants (block grants mainly) constituted 1.5 percent; and general-purpose aid 1.5 percent. By 1977, with the passage of revenue sharing and the creation of additional block-grant programs, categorical aid was down to 76 percent of the total, with broad-based aid making up 10 percent and general-purpose aid (revenue sharing and anti-recession assistance) making up 14 percent (see table 1). Since that time, the percentage of categorical aid has remained about the same, with the percentage of block-grant aid rising and that of revenue sharing falling. In President Carter's fiscal 1982 budget proposals, categorical programs would have received about 78 percent of the federal grant-in-aid total; broad-based aid programs would have received 16.6 percent; and general-purpose aid would have been allotted 6.4 percent.[5]

The Rationale and Purposes of Federal Grants-in-Aid

There are a number of economic, political, and administrative justifications which have been advanced (sometimes in combination) to explain and to provide a theoretical underpinning for the federal grant-in-aid system.

The economic case for federal grants stems largely from a perceived deficiency in the federal fiscal system: the spillover of program

---

[4] Carl W. Stenberg, "Block Grants: The Middlemen of the Federal Aid System," p. 10; David B. Walker, "Categorical Grants: Some Clarifications and Continuing Concerns," *Intergovernmental Perspective* (Spring 1977), p. 16.

[5] ACIR, *Categorical Grants: Their Role and Design*, pp. 15–38; Dale Tate, "New Federalism No Panacea for State and Local Government," *Congressional Quarterly* (April 25, 1981), pp. 708–10.

TABLE 1

FEDERAL AID OUTLAYS, BY TYPE, FISCAL 1968–1977
(in millions of dollars and percent of total)

Type	1968		1972		1975		1977	
General revenue sharing	—		—		$ 6,130	12%	$ 6,758	10%
General support aid	$ 294	2%	$ 490	1.5%	841	2	2,748[a]	4
Block grant[b]	57	—	415	1.5	5,393	11	7,063	10
Categorical grants[c]	18,248	98	35,035	97	37,359	75	51,827[d]	76
Total federal grants	$18,599	100%	$35,940	100%	$49,723	100%	$68,396	100%

[a] Includes $1,699 Antirecession Financial Assistance and $276 federal payment to the District of Columbia.

[b] Includes totals for block grants (Partnership for Health, Safe Streets, Social Services, Comprehensive Employment and Training [CETA], and Community Development), although a portion may be granted for specific projects under the discretionary allocation provided for by statute.

[c] Includes target grants like Model Cities and the Appalachian Regional Commission Program.

[d] Includes funds for two countercyclical programs: Local Public Works—$577, and CETA (Titles II and VI)—$3,524 (est.).

SOURCE: Office of Management and Budget, *Special Analyses; Budget of The United States and Budget Appendix,* (Washington, D.C., various years).

benefits beyond the boundaries of individual states and localities.[6] Thus, federal support for broad general purposes such as interstate highways or environmental protection (waste-water treatment plants) is defended on grounds that the benefits that accrue go beyond the confines of a particular strip of highway or of a community in which the waste treatment plant is built. Local taxpayers, it is argued, having little incentive to pay for benefits that go to others, will generally not give adequate support to these kinds of activities.

In addition, the economic case for federal funding is based on a general fact of life within our federal system: fiscal imbalance. Particularly since the passage of the income tax amendment early in the century, the federal government's taxing system has operated more efficiently and equitably—and has generated more revenue— than taxing systems of state and local governments. Further, states and localities have often been constrained from levying taxes because of fear of losing out to other states and localities in the competition for businesses and residents.

Finally, there is a combined political and socioeconomic rationale for grants to meet the needs of the poor and disadvantaged. Assuming a national consensus that the government must guarantee minimum life support resources for all individuals and a consensus against direct federal payments to individuals or direct federal service delivery, then federal aid to state and local governments is justified by the spillover case noted above. Specifically, in regard to programs for the poor, one analyst has stated that it is "difficult for the average taxpayer in one locality to vote funds for public services that benefit principally the poor if other localities gain a competitive advantage by not taxing themselves to the same extent for these needs."[7]

Political scientists and government officials have often argued the case for grant-in-aid programs as means of achieving broad national purposes. The Commission on Intergovernmental Relations (Kestenbaum Commission) concluded the following in 1955:

> The national government has used the grant-in-aid system primarily to achieve some national objective. . . . Specific objectives have been as varied as getting the farmer out of the mud, assisting the needy aged, providing lunch for schoolchildren and preventing cancer.

[6] George F. Break, *Financing Government in a Federal System*, pp. 73–122; Charles L. Schultze, "Sorting Out the Social Grant Programs: An Economist's Criteria," *American Economic Review (Papers and Proceedings, 1973)*, May 1974, pp. 181–86; ACIR, *Categorical Grants: Their Role and Design*, pp. 50–51.

[7] Charles L. Schultze, "Federal Spending: Past, Present and Future," in Henry Owen and Charles L. Schultze, eds., *Setting National Priorities: The Next Ten Years* (Washington, D.C., 1976), p. 365.

The Kestenbaum Commission, however, went on to posit as a general rule that a grant should be given

> only for a clearly indicated and presently important national objective. This calls for a searching and selective test of the justification for national participation. . . . Where the activity is one normally considered the primary responsibility of state and local governments, substantial evidence should be required that national participation is necessary in order to protect or promote the national interest.[8]

The federal grant system was never wholly confined to areas where there was a "clearly indicated and presently important national objective." But during the 1960s there occurred a sweeping expansion of categorical grant activities into areas that were traditionally state and local responsibilities. In addition, the federal government used the grant system, particularly during the Great Society period, to draw states and localities into new program areas—such as mental health, job training, and remedial education—which were within the traditional fields of activities for these governments but on which they had expended few or no resources. Another use of federal grants was to demonstrate new approaches in the solution of domestic problems. Initial grants provided "seed money," for instance, as the first step in the development of full-scale programs in such areas as mass transit, juvenile delinquency, and prenatal care. Charles Schultze has commented that many of the new categorical programs "probably served no major national purpose but simply reflected the substitution of the judgment of federal legislators and agency officials for that of state and local officials regarding priorities in these areas."[9]

During the Nixon administration, with general revenue sharing, the rationale for federal aid came almost completely full circle: The federal government provided support for no specific substantive national purpose; it merely underwrote the priorities of state and local governments. The Nixon administration justified general revenue sharing both on fiscal and on political grounds. The fiscal rationale was that the revenue systems of the federal government and those of state and local governments were not balanced and the more efficient, progressive federal tax system should be used as a means of general support. The political justification was that this stable source of money would help restore the state and local governments to a stronger position within the federal system and would allow them to set their own priorities without a distorting federal influence.

[8] U.S., Congress, House, Message from the President of the United States, *The Commission on Intergovernmental Relations,* 84th Congress, 1st session, June 28, 1955, p. 119.

[9] Charles L. Schultze, "Federal Spending: Past, Present and Future," p. 367.

One justification of the current grant-in-aid system—particularly with regard to the more flexible block grants and general and special revenue-sharing proposals—is administrative; it is built upon the perceived individual strengths and weaknesses of the federal, state, and local governments. The federal government is the most efficient of the three levels at collecting revenue, and it is the entity which properly should set overall national objectives and goals. Because of the size and complexity of the United States, however, state and local governments are better equipped to administer most domestic programs, particularly those which must take into account regional, economic, or social variations. Often the defense of the existing administrative division of labor is combined with a defense from grounds of political philosophy: that is, a strong preference for a balance of power and authority within the federal system and the belief that state and local governments are more responsive and accountable than the federal government because they operate closer to their citizens.

Regarding administrative decentralization in the United States, ACIR has noted the following:

> Loyalties to the states and a belief in the desirability of strong, independent local communities, probably have promoted the sharing of functions through federal aid rather than a desire for direct national administration. Throughout much of the nation's history, a centralization of power in the national government has been feared and opposed by large segments of the public. Grants-in-aid have had the advantage of permitting a considerable degree of discretion for states and communities to develop service standards, and to administer aided activities.[10]

Theory and Practice

While theoretical explanations can provide an organizing framework for analyzing the federal grant system, it cannot be said that the system began, grew, or functions today as a result of rational, orderly planning or implementation. Often the real explanation behind the creation of a categorical or block-grant program has had little to do with spillover or a proper administrative division of labor but much to do with the personal convictions or political needs of a congressional committee chairman or a president and the narrow goals of a special interest group.

The congressional structure and organization, granting as it does

---

[10] ACIR, *Categorical Grants: Their Role and Design*, p. 52.

extraordinary power to subcommittee chairmen, is more a determinant of grant program creation than any intellectual framework for a rational response to unmet needs. Harold Seidman accurately captured a typical result of the fragmentation of Congress when he recounted:

> It's no accident that we have four different water and sewer (grant) programs, because these come out of four separate committees of Congress. These are very important programs for a Congressman's constituency, and a Congressman wants to be sure that it will remain an agency under the jurisdiction of his committee.[11]

Special interest groups have taken full advantage of congressional fragmentation in pressing a multitude of individual claims, arguing that the needs are real, that rights and entitlements are involved, and that national purposes are being served. Congress, for the past decade, has shied away from massive new social programs, substituting hundreds of narrow-purpose grants for comprehensive reform.

Charles Schultze, in reviewing the rationale and the realities behind the federal grant system, argues that economic theory regarding spillover or externalities is

> not a very useful guide for analyzing most of the existing social grants. . . . Rather many of these grants are a means by which the federal government uses state and local governments . . . as agents or subcontractors to produce centrally determined amounts and kinds of collective goods, since, for a number of reasons, principally historical and political, the federal government virtually never delivers collective goods or services at the local level.[12]

[11] Harold Seidman, quoted in Douglas M. Fox, "A Mini-Symposium: President Nixon's Proposals for Executive Reorganization," *Public Administration Review*, September/October, 1974, p. 489.

[12] Charles L. Schultze, "Sorting Out the Social Grant Programs: An Economist's Criteria," pp. 182–83.

2

American Federalism Today: How We Got Here

American federalism, like most elements of the American political tradition, has always defied precise definition and neat symmetry. Twenty years ago, just at the outset of what were to be two decades of ferment, change, and increasing complexity and confusion within the federal system, Morton Grodzins wrote his now-famous critique of the standard, oversimplified vision of federalism:

> The American form of government is often, but erroneously, symbolized by a three-layer cake. A far more accurate image is the rainbow or marble cake, characterized by an insepar- able mingling of differently colored ingredients, the colors appearing in vertical and diagonal strands and unexpected whirls. As colors are mixed into the marble cake, so func- tions are mixed in the American federal system.[1]

In 1981, there are many more "colors," "ingredients," "strands," and "unexpected whirls" than Grodzins could ever have imagined in 1960.

To some, the complex and confusing attributes of current inter- governmental relations are by no means all bad. Richard P. Nathan, a longtime observer and sometime participant in the system, has stated: "I'll admit to a bias. . . . I think the current federal grant system has a lot of good qualities. It reflects the ability of a federal democracy and a free society to respond flexibly and dynamically to emerging problems. I am not of the 'Henny-Penny, sky is falling' school of federalism."[2]

Conversely, ACIR over the past twenty years, through diligent and able research, has built a powerful indictment of the system,

---

[1] Morton Grodzins, "The Federal System," *Goals for Americans: Programs for Action in the Sixties*, Report of the President's Commission on National Goals and Chapters Submitted for the Consideration of the Commission (Prentice-Hall for the American Assembly, Columbia University, New York, 1960), p. 265.

[2] Richard P. Nathan, lecture delivered at the National Health Policy Forum, Wash- ington, D.C., May 19, 1981.

based upon its "administrative failures, red tape . . . poor performance and inadequate results . . . excessive costs and waste . . . and lack of control and responsiveness."[3] According to its own conclusions, the ACIR might well argue that if it leads the "Henny-Penny" school of federalism, then Nathan and others like him lead the rival "Pollyanna" school.

Before 1960

The paragraphs above illustrate that disagreements over the nature of federalism have ever formed part of the warp and woof of American political debates and that the sweeping proposals lately advanced by the Reagan administration are but the latest in a long series of reinterpretations of the concept and attempts at restructuring the system.

The intergovernmental aid system itself goes far back in our history. The 1836 Surplus Distribution Act, which gave surplus federal funds from land sales to the states, was the first example of federal revenue sharing; and the Morrill Act of 1862, which gave portions of the public domain to states for the support of higher education, constituted the prototype of later federal categorical grants. During the late nineteenth and early twentieth centuries, the federal government gradually expanded the grant-in-aid system, adding programs for agricultural experiment stations, state forestry promotion, merchant marine schools, and highways.

The Great Depression and the New Deal produced major changes in intergovernmental relations—indeed, the term "intergovernmental relations" first came into use during this period. The federal government moved vigorously to expand its activities in the area of social welfare. Sixteen continuing grant-in-aid programs were established between 1933 and 1938; and federal aid to state and local governments, though fluctuating because of temporary programs, increased sharply overall. The peak year was 1935 when $2.2 billion were dispensed to state and local governments, an extraordinary increase when contrasted with the $100 million given out in 1930.[4]

The Social Security Act of 1935 was the most significant single New Deal legislative enactment relating to federal aid, for it created a number of social welfare categorical programs, including old-age

---

[3] ACIR, *The Federal Role in the Federal System: The Dynamics of Growth*, vol. 1, *A Crisis in Confidence and Competence* (Washington, D.C., 1980), pp. 3–30.

[4] ACIR, *Categorical Grants: Their Role and Design* (Washington, D.C., 1978), pp. 17–21; Deil S. Wright, *Federal Grants-in-Aid: Perspectives and Alternatives* (Washington, D.C.: American Enterprise Institute, 1968), pp. 25–34.

assistance, aid to the blind, aid to dependent children, unemployment compensation, and grants for child health, crippled children, and child welfare. When the Supreme Court upheld the constitutionality of the act, it provided a solid, enduring legal foundation for the federal grant-in-aid system to reach into almost any area of domestic concern.

During the Second World War and the decade following, there was a slow but steady increase in federal dollars and grant programs for state and local governments. The most important and innovative grant program of the 1950s came in the Highway Act of 1956, which provided for the creation of the interstate highway system through a system of matching grants (the federal government provided 90 percent of the cost of construction).

1960–1980: The Maturing of the Intergovernmental Grant System

While references to the historical origins of the intergovernmental grant system, and particularly to the experience of the New Deal, are important for a long-term perspective, the real keys to understanding the current grant-in-aid system and the Reagan proposals and the likely reaction to them are to be found in the political history of the last two decades and in the impact that history has had on American federalism. For it has been during the last twenty years that the complex attributes, the intricate interrelationships, and the multiplicity of actors have emerged to form a mature, complicated federal system that, to revert to Grodzins's metaphor, abounds in "colors," "strands," and "unexpected whirls."

Underlying Factors. Before reviewing the history of the past two decades, one should note two underlying factors: the impact of the relatively efficient federal revenue system that continually generated large sums of money for Congress and the executive to dispense and the concomitant widespread hostility to any massive growth in the federal bureaucracy.

The increasing predominance of the federal government in the government revenue field buttressed the expansion of the federal grant system, at least until the late 1970s. Forty years ago, federal revenue accounted for about 10 percent of the Gross National Product (GNP), with state and local revenue combined accounting for 8.5 percent. In 1980, these figures were 22 percent and 11 percent respectively. Today, the federal government raises 56 percent of all public revenue, while the states raise 25 percent and local governments only 19 percent.

The key to the expansion of the federal role in taxation has been the progressive income tax, which now constitutes over two-thirds of general federal tax revenue. Responding positively both to national economic growth and inflation, the income tax has generated ever-increasing sums of money for the federal government to allocate. And during the past two decades, an increasing amount of federal revenue has gone into the intergovernmental aid system. In 1960, intergovernmental fiscal transfers amounted to a little more than $7 billion, less than 2 percent of the GNP and about 15 percent of total state-local outlays. In 1978, the peak year for federal grant spending over the past two decades, federal intergovernmental assistance programs amounted to $83 billion, 3.8 percent of the GNP and 32 percent of all state-local revenue. Since 1978, though the absolute total has risen, federal grants have declined as a percentage of GNP and as a percentage of state-local revenue.[5]

State and local taxes, until recently, were tied to sales and property taxes, which lack the peculiarly escalating characteristics of the progressive income tax. State and local governments faced the politically difficult task of actually legislating tax increases, while Congress could just sit back and allow growth, inflation, and "bracket creep" to generate increasing revenue.

During the past decade, state and local revenues—particularly state revenues, as many states have reformed and diversified their tax systems—have risen substantially; but they have not been able to keep pace with the demands and costs of domestic services such as education, welfare, health, police and fire protection, parks and recreation, and housing. Thus, there has occurred what some economists have called a "fiscal mismatch" between the demands for social services and the varying abilities of the federal, state, and local taxing systems to meet those demands. Specifically, as one researcher has noted, "Our intergovernmental revenue system suffers from a fiscal capacity to . . . need mismatch which has led to the need for massive transfers of money from the federal government, which raises the money, to local governments which spend it."[6]

Though the federal role in domestic program areas expanded greatly between 1960 and 1980, there was no corresponding increase in the federal bureaucracy (see table 2). The number of civilian federal

[5] George F. Break, *Financing Government in a Federal System*, pp. 1–11; Catherine H. Lovell, "Federal Assistance to Local Governments and Its Conditions," paper for conference: *The Federal Purse: The Role of Law*, (Washington, D.C.: Smithsonian Institution, March 12, 1981); ACIR, *Significant Features of Fiscal Federalism, 1979–1980 Edition* (Washington, D.C., 1980), pp. 161–62.

[6] Catherine H. Lovell, "Federal Assistance to Local Governments and Its Conditions," p. 4.

TABLE 2

GROWTH IN NUMBER OF PUBLIC EMPLOYEES, 1929–1979
(thousands)

As of October	Total Public Sector	Federal	State	Local
1929	3,100	600	600	1,900
1939	4,200	1,100	700	2,400
1944	6,537	3,365	700	2,472
1949	6,203	2,047	1,037	3,119
1954	7,232	2,373	1,149	3,710
1959	8,487	2,399	1,454	4,634
1964	10,064	2,528	1,873	5,663
1969	12,685	2,969	2,614	7,102
1970	13,028	2,881	2,755	7,392
1971	13,316	2,872	2,832	7,612
1972	13,603	2,795	2,938	7,870
1973	14,139	2,786	3,013	8,339
1974	14,668	2,874	3,155	8,639
1975	14,986	2,890	3,268	8,828
1976	15,012	2,843	3,343	8,826
1977	15,459	2,848	3,481	9,130
1978	15,631	2,888	3,539	9,204
1979 (est.)	15,755	2,895	3,590	9,270

SOURCE: U.S. Bureau of the Census, *Public Employment*, annually; and estimates of the staff of the Advisory Commission on Intergovernmental Regulations.

employees—2.9 million—is only slightly larger today than it was two decades ago. During the same period, however, the number of state and local government employees went up dramatically, now standing at about 3.6 million for state and 9.3 million for local government employees. Further, it has been estimated that about 5 million state, local, and private-sector employees constitute a pool of indirect federal employees—that is, employees whose salaries are paid indirectly by the federal government through grants and contracts, even though they are not under federal jurisdiction and control.[7]

Thus, while the federal government has continually enlarged the scope of its activities over the past two decades, it has increasingly been dependent on others—state and local governments and the

[7] ACIR, *In Brief: The Federal Role in the Federal System* (Washington, D.C., 1980), p. 8; ACIR, *A Crisis in Confidence and Competence*, pp. 131–33, 149.

private and nonprofit sectors—to carry out its purposes. As ACIR has stated: "Massive intergovernmental assistance programs are the basic means by which national policymakers have been able to keep the federal bureaucracy relatively small while still ostensibly accomplishing federal purposes."[8]

The Great Society. From 1964 through 1969, the Great Society produced an explosion in the number of federal grants, a sizable increase in the federal dollars going into those grants, and a substantial change in their programmatic distribution.

Reflecting the social and economic goals of the Johnson administration, the federal government in partnership with state and local governments and with the private sector took on many new social and urban problems—poverty, disease, unemployment, illiteracy, racial injustice, crime, substandard housing, and urban physical decay.

Under the title "creative federalism," the chief vehicle for the achievement of these expanded federal goals and purposes was the grant-in-aid system. During the Johnson presidency, some 240 new categorical aid programs were created, 109 being enacted in one year (1965) alone. The functional distribution of federal aid also changed dramatically, reflecting the new social priorities: Commerce and transportation programs dropped from 36 percent to 23 percent between 1963 and 1968, while health and human resources programs increased from 13 percent to 40 percent during the same period.[9]

There are two phenomena associated with, or resulting from, the Great Society era that have had, and will continue to have, an enduring effect on subsequent attempts to revise the intergovernmental aid system. The first relates to the so-called iron triangle of special interest groups allied with executive agency specialists and congressional subcommittees or committees. Iron triangles certainly did not originate with the Great Society; but, with the creation of over two hundred new categorical programs during a five-year span, they did become more broadly and deeply entrenched within the intergovernmental aid system. In a real sense, what occurred was a democratizing of the existing iron triangle system in that newer groups—blacks and other minorities, the handicapped, the elderly, consumers, welfare recipients, children's advocates—were consciously fostered and protected by Great Society reformers with the

[8] ACIR, *In Brief: The Federal Role in the Federal System,* p. 9.
[9] David B. Walker, "Categorical Grants: Some Clarifications and Continuing Concerns," *Intergovernmental Perspective* (Spring 1977), p. 15; ACIR, *Categorical Grants: Their Role and Design,* p. 25.

aim of bringing them fully and permanently into the political process. These groups in turn became the most vigilant guardians of their particular categorical grant, their "piece of the action."

Not only did the architects of the Great Society consciously foster new interest groups for the poor and the minorities, but in a number of cases they created grant programs that bypassed state and local elected officials and established direct connections with local community groups and nonprofit organizations or forced the creation of a new quasi-public structure (for instance Model Cities agencies) that operated beyond the effective control of state or local governments. The Economic Opportunity Act—and the 850 community-action organizations it spawned—represents the most famous case in point, but a number of programs now provide direct aid to a whole new substratum of community-based groups, neighborhood groups, and groups with specialized functional interests in such areas as migrant health, family planning, low-income housing, and rural social services. This direct federal grant–private organization connection constitutes a second enduring inheritance from the late 1960s, one that will have to be reckoned with in any revamping of the existing system.

The New Federalism. The Nixon administration set out consciously to reverse many of the trends in federalism that had been dominant over the previous thirty years. To that end, the president proposed general revenue sharing to provide a permanent source of broad fiscal support for state and local governments; six special revenue-sharing grants would allow state and local governments maximum flexibility to administer programs in the areas of education, law enforcement, manpower training, rural community development, urban community development, and transportation. Partly because of the rapid decline in the administration's power and authority after Watergate, Congress only enacted general revenue sharing and watered-down legislation in the community development and manpower areas.

In defending the new federalism proposals, the Nixon administration employed arguments and rhetoric strikingly similar to that put forward today by the Reagan administration. The federal government had taken on too many responsibilities and was incapable of solving the nation's domestic problems. The time had come to sort out the appropriate roles and responsibilities of each level of government. The system of categorical grants was duplicative, wasteful, and plagued with too many federal strings. And state and local elected officials were best capable of defining their own needs and priorities.

Though Watergate thwarted the major federalism goals of the Nixon administration, Congress did enact three additional block grant proposals between 1973 and 1975: the Comprehensive Employment and Training Act (1973), the Housing and Community Development Act (1974), and the Title XX amendments to the Social Security Act of 1935 (1975). Two previous block grants, the Partnership for Health and the Safe Streets Act, had been passed during the Johnson administration. In 1976 President Ford proposed four additional block grants in the areas of health, education, child nutrition, and social services, but Congress ignored his requests.

By the end of the Ford administration, then, the tripartite federal-grant system was fully in place: general support for state and local governments with general revenue sharing; broad-based support for large functional program areas with the five block-grant programs; and finally narrowly targeted support with hundreds of categorical grants.

During the 1970s, though Congress consistently refused to tackle major social reforms (in the welfare and health-financing areas for instance), it continued to expand the range and number of smaller scale categorical programs. From 1970 to 1980, about 200 new categorical grants were created (bringing the total to around 600) and by the end of the decade there was almost no state or local activity—from library administration and art education to pothole repair and boating safety—that had not been penetrated by federal dollars. The lines between national issues and subnational issues were all but obliterated as the nation entered the 1980s. (See table 3 for categorical grants broken down by functional area.)

Continuing Results of Revenue Sharing. As with the Great Society experience, there emerged from the Nixon-Ford new-federalism years certain lasting phenomena that would have a direct impact on later attempts to change the federal grant system.

From the point of intergovernmental relations, the most important consequence of general revenue sharing was to bring thousands of general purpose local governments into direct participation with the federal aid system. (The Nixon administration had been wary of this result; but, in order to gain political support from the mayors and county officials for revenue sharing, it had decided to allow local governments to receive revenue-sharing funds directly.) The Comprehensive Employment and Training Act (CETA) and the commu-

TABLE 3

CATEGORICAL GRANT PROGRAMS, 1978

Budget Subfunction	Number of Programs
Department of Defense—Military	5
General Science and Basic Research	1
Energy	6
Water Resources	7
Conservation and Land Management	13
Recreational Resources	10
Pollution Control and Abatement	35
Other Natural Resources	4
Agricultural Research and Services	9
Mortgage Credit and Thrift Insurance	2
Other Advancement and Regulation of Commerce	2
Ground Transportation	36
Water Transportation	2
Mass Transportation	8
Air Transportation	3
Other Transportation	1
Community Development	5
Area and Regional Development	36
Disaster Relief and Insurance	9
Elementary, Secondary, and Vocational Education	70
Higher Education	10
Research and General Education Aids	21
Training and Employment	23
Other Labor Services	1
Social Services	47
Health	78
Public Assistance and Other Income Supplements	27
Hospital and Medical Care for Veterans	5
Criminal Justice Assistance	13
General Property and Records Management	1
Other General Government	2
Total	492

SOURCE: Advisory Commission on Intergovernmental Regulations.

nity development block-grant program further added to the number of local general- and special-purpose units directly dependent on some amount of federal aid, and today it is estimated that some 65,000 units of subnational government (four-fifths of the total) receive federal grants. Further, whereas twenty years ago only 8 percent of federal aid went to local governments directly, in 1980 about 25 percent did so. The ACIR has estimated that in 1978 direct federal grants to the nation's forty-seven largest cities equaled about 50 percent of the money these cities raised locally from their own tax systems.[10] (See table 4.) If welfare grants (Aid to Families with Dependent Children [AFDC] and Medicare) are eliminated from consideration, almost half the federal aid to states and localities now goes directly to local governments.

In addition to the large increase in local government participation, thousands of regional and subnational bodies were created largely through federal directives. These included over 2,000 substate regional planning bodies, some 500 clearinghouses for handling areawide comment on and review of grant programs under an Office of Management and Budget (OMB) circular, several multistate economic development commissions, and ten federal regional councils.[11]

The increasingly strong umbilical ties between the cities and the federal government served to highlight a second important phenomenon: the continual bypassing and downgrading of the role of the states. The deterioration of the position of the states in the federal system did not begin in the early 1970s with revenue sharing. The New Deal had created a kind of watershed in federal-state relations, leaving the states with a smaller role in many domestic program areas. The trend of bypassing the states accelerated during the years of the Great Society when the states were given virtually no role in the antipoverty, Model Cities, and other urban-development and social-reform programs passed during the Johnson administration. Though increasingly belied by the facts, the common view of state governments in the early 1970s was that they were unrepresentative, corrupt, inept, and racist.

Whatever the shifts in the balance of power and influence, both state and local governments sought to shape policy at the seat of power in Washington. Thus, during the 1960s and 1970s, along with an increase in the number of functional special interest groups came stepped-up activities by the associations representing various elements of state and local governments: governors, state legislators, mayors, city councilmen, county executives, and city managers. With large staffs, these organizations, in an age of computer grantsman-

[10] Richard P. Nathan, "Federal Grants—How Are They Working?" in Robert W. Burchell and David Listokin, eds., *Cities Under Stress: The Fiscal Crises of Urban America* (New Brunswick, N.J.: Rutgers University Press, 1981),pp. 529–30; Carl W. Stenberg, "Federalism in Transition: 1959–1979," *Intergovernmental Perspective* (Winter 1980), p. 6; ACIR, *In Brief: The Federal Role in the Federal System: The Dynamics of Growth*, (Washington, D.C., 1980), p. 8.

[11] Carl W. Stenberg, "Federalism in Transition: 1959–1979," p. 12.

TABLE 4

STATE AND LOCAL RELIANCE ON OUTSIDE AID, 1948–1978

Fiscal Year	Federal Aid to States		State and Federal Aid to Local Governments	
	Amount (millions of dollars)	As percentage of state general revenue from own sources	Amount (millions of dollars)	As percentage of local general revenue from own sources
1948	1,643	21.9	3,501	44.5
1954	2,668	21.5	5,933	43.5
1959	5,888	32.4	8,739	42.2
1964	9,046	32.1	13,829	45.7
1969	16,907	34.1	26,082	56.9
1970	19,252	33.5	29,525	57.5
1971	22,754	37.1	34,473	60.0
1972	26,791	37.9	39,694	60.6
1973	31,361[a]	39.0	47,866[a]	67.9
1974	31,632[a]	35.5	54,752[a]	71.3
1975	36,148[a]	37.3	61,975[a]	73.5
1976	42,013[a]	39.1	69,746[a]	74.8
1977	45,938[a]	37.9	76,948[a]	75.4
1978 (est.)	53,000[a]	38.8	85,500[a,b]	76.8

[a] Includes the following federal general revenue-sharing payments (in billions): 1973—state $2.2, local $4.4; 1974—state $2.0, local $4.1; 1975—state $2.0, local $4.1; 1976—state $2.1, local $4.1; 1977—state $2.3, local $4.4; 1978—state $2.3, local $4.5.

[b] The $85.5 billion of intergovernmental aid received by local governments in 1978 can be broken down as follows: $20.5 billion direct federal aid, approximately $15 billion indirect federal aid (passed through the state and estimated on the basis of 1967 data, the latest available), and $50.0 billion direct state aid.

SOURCE: ACIR staff compilation based on U.S. Bureau of the Census, *Governmental Finances*, various years, and ACIR staff estimates.

ship, could quickly calculate to the penny how cities and states would fare under any proposed changes in the intergovernmental grant system.

Finally, there was a third phenomenon which all participants in the federal grant-in-aid system began to feel acutely during the 1970s: the increasing scope and number of federal regulations that accompanied federal largesse. Indeed, one of the ironic consequences of general revenue sharing—which aimed to give maximum flexibility to state and local officials—was the unintended snaring of state and local governments in the complex web of federal regulations. In 1960 few strings were attached to federal grants. Today it is estimated that the federal government imposes 1,259 mandates on state and local governments, 223 of which are direct orders and the rest (1,036) conditions of aid. Fifty-nine of these mandates constitute crosscutting regulations (relating, for instance, to such matters as civil rights, environmental protection, and merit staffing) which apply to most federal grants regardless of their specific purpose. According to state and local officials, the situation has worsened since the mid-1970s because Congress, faced with persistent budget crunches, has tended to substitute regulatory mandates for dollars.[12]

Thus, by the end of the 1970s, the intergovernmental grant-in-aid system had evolved into an incredible maze, with numerous actors and special interests, complicated structural interrelationships, and inconsistent functional division of authority among the three levels of government. Any attempt to reform or simplify the system would inevitably disturb this complex balance and arouse both anxiety and suspicion.

The Carter Administration: A Watershed. Though Ronald Reagan's victory over Jimmy Carter in November 1980 will no doubt be counted as a historic turning point, many of the factors that led to that turning point were evident during the four years of the Carter administration. Persistent, pervasive inflation produced a genuine grassroots revolt against spending and taxes that resulted in Proposition 13 in California and the more draconian Proposition 2½ in Massachusetts. Calls for constitutional amendments to limit spending and force balanced budgets were repeatedly aired in Congress and in state legislatures.

All of these events had a direct impact on the federal grant-in-aid system. During the Carter administration there occurred a major slowdown and then a decline in the growth of intergovernmental aid. Between 1970 and 1975, federal aid (in real dollars) to state and local governments grew at an average of 11.1 percent per year. In 1977–1978, federal aid was down to 5.9 percent; in 1978–1979, it was -1.6 percent; and in 1980–1981, it was -5 percent. Further, the federal budget squeeze produced a major battle when general revenue shar-

---

[12] ACIR, *A Crisis in Confidence and Competence*, pp. 46–47; Catherine H. Lovell and others, *Federal and State Mandating on Local Governments: An Exploration of Issues and Impacts*, a Report to the National Science Foundation (Riverside, Calif.: University of California, 1979); William E. Hudson, "The New Federalism Paradox," *Policy Studies Journal* (Summer 1980), pp. 900–906.

ing came up for renewal in 1980, with the result that the states were cut out of the program entirely during the first year of reauthorization and the future funding level for local governments, in real terms, will be far below that of the 1970s.[13]

[13] Richard P. Nathan, "Reforming the Federal Grants-in-Aid System for States and Localities," Address delivered to the National Tax Association (Washington, D.C., May 18, 1981).

3

Reagan Federalism: Initial Goals

No administration during its first year in office can be expected to have all of its arguments and governing theories finely honed, but Reagan administration officials have developed a tentative but firmly articulated set of administrative, constitutional, and political defenses for the president's goals regarding federalism and the division of responsibilities among the federal, state, and local governments. Possibly the advanced state of their thinking stems from the fact that Reagan himself has held a number of these views since entering public life in the 1960s.

The following discussion and analysis is distilled from testimony and public statements by administration officials and from interviews with administration appointees who have had major responsibilities in developing the president's block-grant proposals and who are very involved in the planning for future initiatives in the intergovernmental relations area—Robert B. Carleson, special assistant to the president for Human Resources and Donald W. Moran, associate director of the Office of Management and Budget for Human Resources.

The Federal and State Roles

Regarding the role of the federal government in domestic affairs, Carleson stated: "The first question is whether there should be any government involvement at all at any level. If an idea or program passes that test, then we basically set up a whole system of burdens of proof. Why isn't this a local problem? Why is this a state problem? Only after going through those hoops will we consider it in relation to other federal priorities."[1] Moran answered the same question from a different perspective:

> We revert to the line of reasoning of most economists; it becomes a national issue only when clearly and unambig-

---

[1] Interview by the author with Robert B. Carleson, special assistant to the president for human resources, May 19, 1981. The subsequent quotations by Carleson in the text are all from this interview.

uously everybody benefits. That, plus the general constitutional presumption that the national government is mainly
responsible for defense and those matters which have any
direct impact on interstate commerce, gives us a pretty good
guide to weed out many subnational issues and programs.[2]

Moran mentioned research and development, the legal system, interstate highways, and immunization programs as examples of areas
in which one could clearly establish an "unambiguous national public
good."

The administration has set out to reverse the trend of decline
in influence and authority of the state governments. Moran stated:
"It is time that the states were brought back into the mainstream.
For too long they have been excluded and bypassed. The president
intends to restore to them their rightful consitutional authority and
responsibilities in the federal system."

Responding to a statement before the House Manpower and
Housing Subcommittee that the administration's block-grant proposals would greatly intensify political struggles at the state level,
Office of Management and Budget (OMB) Director David Stockman
replied: "Yes, and that's good. We are overloaded at the national
level. We simply can't make wise decisions on the thousands of
issues that come before us. There has to be a better division of labor
and a redelegation of decisionmaking to lower levels of government."[3]

Administration officials foresee a substantial diminution of the
direct relationship that has grown up in the last decade between
local governments and Washington. Said Moran: "The local governments should look to their state governments and not to us. They
are the creatures of the states and not of the federal government."

The administration is keenly aware that formal devolution of
programmatic authority will not succeed in the long run unless the
political system is also decentralized. Carleson stated: "We have
consciously set out to force political decisions and the struggles that
accompany them down to the state and local level. The so-called
iron triangles in Washington for too long have had a virtual monopoly on political influence in Congress and in the agencies." He also
noted that, besides making sense from an efficiency and budgetary
angle, the block grants would act to "decouple" particular interest

[2] Interview by the author with Donald W. Moran, associate director of the Office of
Management and Budget for Human Resources, May 12, 1981. The subsequent quotations by Moran in the text are all from this interview.
[3] David A. Stockman, director of the Office of Management and Budget (OMB), testimony before the House Subcommittee on Manpower and Housing, April 28, 1981.

groups from particular programs. "The highly paid Washington representatives are going to scream," he said, "but the interest groups would be well advised to begin beefing up their staff and resources at the fifty state capitals."

Carleson argued that the result would be a "more democratic and representative system."

It is a lot easier for the poor or elderly to take a crosstown bus to city hall or a train to the state capitol than it is for them to come to Washington. It's at the state and local level that they can exert really influential pressure—as a former city manager, I know what it's like to face a stream of taxpayers just on the other side of your desk—you listen and act if you want to keep your job.

Short- and Long-Range Goals

Because the administration's first order of business in January was to reduce federal spending drastically, the initial defense of the block-grant proposals has been skewed toward that goal. OMB Deputy Director Edwin L. Harper told the Senate Subcommittee on Intergovernmental Relations on May 13, 1981:

The block grant designs must be viewed in the context of the total budget. To accomplish the goals of the Economic Recovery Program, it was clear that an immediate reduction in the growth of federal assistance was essential. In order for the states to ensure that these reductions could occur *without causing reduction in service levels* [italics added], we quickly realized that massive reductions in program prescriptiveness and administrative requirements had to accompany budget cuts. Our block grant proposals are designed to satisfy this objective.[4]

The administration proposed a 25 percent reduction in the programs slotted for block grants, but administration officials since January have been cautious not to predict, as Harper did, no "reduction in service levels." More typical was the response of OMB Associate Director Moran: "We don't have an exact figure, but we are certain that the states will be better off with the flexibility and absence of federal prescriptions in the block grant than they would have been with the regulations that go with the eighty-odd categoricals they are replacing."

Over the long run, the block grants themselves represent only

---

[4] Edwin L. Harper, deputy director of the Office of Management and Budget, testimony before the Senate Subcommittee on Intergovernmental Relations, May 13, 1981.

a first step toward turning over full authority, with accompanying resources, to state governments in a number of domestic program areas. Said Carleson: "The block grants represent a kind of halfway house. The president's ultimate goal is to give up control and authority for many domestic program areas—along with appropriate taxing authority—to the states. The federal government will be confined to those issues that are truly national in scope."

The administration, Carleson stated, had no fixed position on a particular division of responsibilities or on how the taxing authority would be shared. "We are open to all kinds of ideas," he said. "We've got a number of people in the administration working on this, and we've asked ACIR to carry out a number of studies for us."

Asked about the ACIR and the National Governors Association (NGA), which have called for a new "sorting out" or redivision of responsibilities by program area between the state and national governments, Moran noted: "Well, if you look at our budget priority projections, you'll see that we've already started a sorting out—just holding the block grants at constant funding fiscal 1982 for the next four years represents a sizable decrease and, therefore, a substantial revision of priorities."

The Tax Turnback Approach

In meetings with state and local government officials, President Reagan has often suggested that his ultimate goal, along with turning over a number of program areas, is to turn back to the states certain federal taxes.

There are several ways that tax turnbacks could be instituted. The federal government could share a percentage of a particular tax— the income tax or one of the excise taxes such as the gasoline tax, the cigarette tax, or the liquor tax—with the states. Another technique would allow the states to pick up a relinquished federal tax base by a 100 percent federal tax credit, up to a limit, for a simultaneous tax imposed by the state. The state, rather than the federal government, would get the revenue, while the taxpayers' combined federal and state tax bills would remain the same.[5]

If the president persists in his belief that the tax turnback route is the way to go, then undoubtedly the idea will be seriously considered at some point by Congress. But because of difficult issues

[5] ACIR Staff, "A Briefing Report: Revenue and Tax Turnbacks," in *Docket Book*, 73rd Meeting (Washington, D.C., April 22–23, 1981); Albert J. Davis and John Shannon, "Stage Two: Revenue Turnbacks," *Intergovernmental Perspective* (Spring 1981), pp. 18–25.

of equity and politics, tax turnbacks will face formidable, possibly insurmountable, obstacles; and it is more likely that the sorting out of responsibilities, as called for by the nation's governors and the ACIR, will emerge as the next step after block grants.

Serious equity questions regarding tax turnbacks arise because there will inevitably be substantial mismatches between the revenue individual states pay for the taxes that are turned back and the needs of those slated for federal aid. (For local governments, the mismatch is even more severe.) Agreement upon a formula to overcome this mismatch—or more importantly agreement upon the criteria and weighting of such a formula—would present major difficulties that would undoubtedly create fierce divisions between individual states, between regions, and between cities and states.

Politically, the administration would likely get caught in a cross-fire between liberals in Congress who would want to keep the federal dollars at the federal level in order to finance social or economic reform programs and fiscal conservatives who would object to this significant separation of taxing from spending responsibilities.

Finally, the administration is committed to a substantial increase in the defense budget, and it will face rising costs of the entitlements in the "safety net" programs it has vowed to protect. It has also combined a promise of tax cuts with a commitment to end deficit spending. The heavy and unrelenting pressures on the federal budget for the foreseeable future form a poor backdrop or basis for proposals to return federal taxes to the states and localities.

The Reagan Block-Grant Proposals

For fiscal 1982, the administration proposed to consolidate all or part of eighty-three categorical programs into six human services block grants, totaling about $11 billion collectively. At the same time, it sought to cut the authorized level of funding for each of the consolidated programs by 25 percent.

The total federal grant outlay to state and local governments for fiscal 1982 would be $86.4 billion, down 13.5 percent from the Carter administration's $99.8 billion. The Reagan budget would have boosted the percentage of grant-in-aid funds allotted to block grants to 38 percent, up from 16.6 percent in the Carter budget.[6]

[6] Executive Office of the President, Office of Management and Budget, *Fiscal Year 1982 Budget Revisions* (Washington, D.C., March 1981), p. 135; Dale Tate, "New Federalism No Panacea for State and Local Governments," *Congressional Quarterly* (April 25, 1981), pp. 708–10.

The six proposed human services block grants were as follows:[7]

1. *Health Services Block Grant.* The health services block-grant proposal consolidated 17 federal health service programs now administered by the Department of Health and Human Services. The programs to be consolidated, among others, included community and migrant health centers, maternal and child health services, mental health and substance abuse programs, home health, emergency medical and hemophilia services, and the sudden infant death syndrome program. A funding authorization of $1.1 billion was requested for each fiscal year from 1982 through 1985.

2. *Preventive Health Services Block Grant.* The preventive health services block-grant proposal consolidated eleven federal health promotion and disease and injury prevention programs administered by the Department of Health and Human Services. The programs included high blood pressure control, health incentive grants, risk education, health education, fluoridation, lead-based paint poisoning prevention, family planning services, venereal disease, rat control, genetic diseases, and adolescent health services. A funding authorization of $242 million was requested for fiscal years 1982 through 1985.

3. *Social Services Block Grant.* The social services block-grant proposal brought together twelve federal social service programs presently administered by three federal agencies: the Department of Health and Human Services, the Department of Education, and the Community Services Administration. The programs included Title XX (an existing social services block grant), child welfare services, foster care,

[7] See appendix B for more details. For detailed analyses of the block grants, both individually and as a group, see the following: Richard S. Schweiker, secretary of the Department of Health and Human Services, testimony before the Senate Committee on Labor and Human Resources (health block grants), April 2, 1981, and before the House Committee on Education and Labor (social services and emergency assistance block grants), March 31, 1981; Terrel H. Bell, secretary of education, testimony before the Senate Subcommittee on Education (education block grants); and David A. Stockman, OMB director, testimony before the House Subcommittee on Manpower and Housing (general defense of block-grant approach, and details on emergency assistance block grant), April 28, 1981.

For analyses outside the administration, see Jule M. Sugarman, "Human Services in the 1980s: A White Paper for Citizens and Government Officials," U.S. Council for the International Year of Disabled Persons, mimeographed (Washington, D.C., May 15, 1981); Ad Hoc Coalition on Block Grants, "Block Grant Briefing Book," mimeographed (Washington, D.C., 1981); Thomas R. Ascik, "Block Grants and Federalism: Decentralizing Decisions," mimeographed (Washington, D.C.: Heritage Foundation, June 5, 1981).

adoption assistance, child abuse, runaway youth, developmental disabilities, rehabilitation services, and community services. An annual funding authorization of $3.8 billion was requested for fiscal years 1982 through 1985.

4. Energy and Emergency Assistance Block Grant. The energy and emergency assistance block grant consolidated two federal programs administered by the Department of Health and Human Services: the low-income energy and the emergency assistance programs. An annual funding authorization of $1.4 billion was requested for fiscal years 1982 through 1985.

5. Local Education Services Block Grant. The local education block grant consolidated twelve federal education programs now administered by the Department of Education. These included financial assistance to meet the special needs of educationally deprived children, handicapped children, children in schools undergoing desegregation, migrant children, and adults lacking basic educational skills. Most funds were to be passed through to local educational agencies, though the states would determine local allocations. A funding authorization of $3.8 billion was requested for fiscal year 1982, with a 5 percent increase each year thereafter until 1985.

6. State Education Services Block Grant. The state education services block grant consolidated over thirty current categorical programs that aim to help states improve school performance and the use of resources. A funding authorization of $565 million was requested for fiscal 1982, with a 5 percent increase for each year thereafter until 1985.

General Characteristics of Reagan Block Grants

The Reagan administration consolidation proposals, though labeled block grants, more closely resembled President Nixon's special revenue-sharing bills of 1971 than they did existing block grants. There were far fewer requirements than are evident in the existing block grants and, within the program boundaries of each consolidation, maximum flexibility and freedom of action were given to the states. For instance, there were no provisions for matching funds by the states, no earmarking of particular categories (except for several years in the local education block grant), and no requirement that the states maintain an existing level of effort or funding for a particular program (again with the exception of the local education grant). In addition, funds for the grant would go directly to the state as an entitlement with no requirement for submission to a federal agency of a state plan for their allocation.

State allotments were based on project and formula grant funds received by the state and the public and private entities within it in fiscal year 1981. Each state, thus, would get a percentage of block-grant funds equal to its share of the total fiscal 1981 appropriations for the programs being consolidated less 25 percent. The state was allowed to reallocate up to 10 percent of each block grant among the other five human services block grants.

The grant funds would go to the governor or any other entity (the legislative or executive departments) designated by state law and would be disbursed in keeping with procedures that the states themselves put in place. The state would have complete freedom to allocate resources within the prescribed program areas within the grant—including zero funding for some existing categorical programs or greatly expanded funding for others.

The states were required to publicize their plans for spending the grant funds and to provide opportunity for public comment, although they were not required to hold formal public hearings. The states also had to prepare reports, at least once every two years, on how the funds were actually used, and they had to provide biennially for an independent audit of grant expenditures. There was, however, no authority for the relevant federal agency to set data guidelines or regulations for uniformity.

Discrimination on the basis of race, color, national origin, sex, age, or handicap was prohibited, with the relevant departmental secretary given oversight and the authority to refer complaints to the attorney general.

Finally, the block-grant proposals repealed over sixty laws or sections of laws that created the eighty-three categorical programs being consolidated.[8]

There are two initial points stemming from the general characteristics of the Reagan block grants that should be underscored. First, freezing the total state dollar allotments at the current categorical grant level postpones facing but does not resolve difficult political and substantive issues that relate to the equitable division of federal dollars among states and localities in the social service, education, and health areas being consolidated. The administration wisely gave itself and Congress several years to attempt to work out reasonable formulas and accommodations in these areas.

[8] Jule M. Sugarman, "Human Services in the 1980s: A White Paper for Citizens and Government Officials," pp. 65–77.

30

Second, federally created incentives that have changed and distorted state and local governments' spending and taxing patterns would have been substantially altered had Congress agreed to the original Reagan block-grant proposals. There would have been fewer of the dollar allocation features that stimulated state and local government spending, such as open-ended cost reimbursement and matching and maintenance of effort requirements.

Congressional Action on Block Grants

Congress made substantial changes in both the form and the substance of the original Reagan administration block-grant proposals. In general, these changes placed limitations on state discretionary action and removed from the block grants a number of the most important categorical programs, while increasing the number of individual block grants.[9]

In the health area, Congress created four block grants in place of the two large-scale consolidations recommended by the president.

1. *Alcohol, Drug Abuse, and Mental Health.* The block grant consolidates alcohol, drug abuse, and community mental health programs. The funding authorization for the consolidated programs is $491 million in fiscal 1982; $511 million in fiscal 1983; and $532 million in fiscal 1984. The fiscal 1982 amount is 25 percent less than the fiscal 1981 funding level. The states are required to fund each of the community mental health centers currently being supported by the federal government, and there is extensive earmarking of funds within the block grant—the states must use at least 35 percent of the funds for alcohol programs, at least 35 percent for drug abuse services, and at least 20 percent for prevention and early intervention programs.

2. *Health Prevention and Services.* This block grant consolidates the following programs: home health services, rodent control, fluoridation, health education and risk reduction, health incentive grants, emergency medical services, rape crisis, and hypertension. Funding is authorized for $95 million in fiscal 1982; $96.5 million in fiscal 1983; and $98.5 million for fiscal 1984 (plus $3 million per year set aside for rape crisis). The fiscal 1982 amount is 25 percent less than the fiscal 1981 level.

3. *Primary Care.* The community health centers program is the sole

---

[9] The material relating to congressional action on the block grants came from two sources: National Governors Association, "Governors Bulletin," July 24 and July 31, 1981; and National Governors Association, "The Impact of the Omnibus Budget Reconciliation Act of 1981 (HR 3982) on the States," mimeographed, Washington, D.C., 1981.

component of this block grant. The funding authorization is for $284 million in fiscal 1982; $302 million in fiscal 1983; and $327 million in fiscal 1984. The fiscal 1982 amount is the same as the fiscal 1981 funding level.

4. *Maternal and Child Health.* Programs concerned with lead-based paint, rehabilitation services, sudden infant death syndrome, hemophilia, genetic diseases, and adolescent health services are consolidated in this block grant. For fiscal 1982, 15 percent of the money is earmarked for special projects of national or regional significance, hemophilia disease centers, and genetic disease programs. The funding for fiscal 1982, 1983, and 1984 is $373 million. The fiscal 1982 level is about 13 percent below the total for the individual categorical programs in fiscal 1981.

While creating four block grants in the health area, Congress, over the strong objections of the administration, retained a number of important and sizable health programs as separate authorizations. Among the existing health programs that remained categorical grants were: migrant health ($43 million), family planning ($143 million), immunization ($29.5 million), venereal disease control ($40 million), development disabilities ($61 million), and adolescent family life ($30 million).

In the social services area, Congress gutted the administration's proposal for a significant melding of programs into one block grant. The sole advance in flexibility from the point of view of the administration and the states was the dropping of the existing matching and maintenance of effort requirement for states in the existing Title XX block grant. The Title XX block grant was authorized at a level of $2.4 billion in fiscal 1982; $2.45 billion in fiscal 1983; $2.5 billion in fiscal 1984; $2.6 billion in fiscal 1985; and $2.7 billion in fiscal 1986. The 1982 level represents a 20 percent reduction from the 1981 level of the incorporated programs.

Congress refused to include in the block grant (as proposed by the administration) the following categorical programs: child abuse ($7 million), runaway youth ($10 million), developmental disabilities ($51 million), rehabilitation services ($931 million), adoption assistance ($10 million), child welfare services ($163 million), and foster care ($349 million).

In addition, the Community Services Administration, which the administration had proposed to fold into the social services block grant, was dismantled but placed in a separate block grant to be administered by the Department of Health and Human Services. The annual authorized funding level for this new block grant is $389.4 million for fiscal 1982 through 1986.

Regarding education, the administration had proposed a state block grant and one for local education agencies (composed largely of programs from Title I of the Elementary and Secondary Education Act). Congress did consolidate into a single grant some thirty small state education programs that are designed to improve school performance and the use of resources. This block grant was authorized at a level of $589 million in fiscal years 1982, 1983, and 1984.

Congress, however, refused to fold into one local education agency block grant the most important Title I programs such as emergency school aid ($108 million), education for the handicapped ($922 million), and adult and vocational education programs ($120 million). These programs will continue as separate categorical grants. Title I is authorized to be funded at a level of $3.48 billion for fiscal years 1982, 1983, and 1984.

Finally, Congress did not go along with the administration's proposal to consolidate two programs—low-income energy assistance and AFDC emergency assistance—into one energy and emergency assistance block grant administered by the Department of Health and Human Services. Congress created a home energy assistance program at a funding level of $1.875 billion for fiscal 1982, 1983, and 1984. Up to 15 percent of that money may be used for the Energy Department's low-income weatherization program, and up to 10 percent may be used for any of the health and social services block grants.

Title XVII of the reconciliation bill (HR 3982) established a series of requirements for the states that pertained to all of the block grants in the bill. First, the states are required to prepare a report that includes a statement of goals and objectives, information on the activities to be supported and the individuals to be served, and the criteria and method for distributing the funds. Second, the states must hold public hearings on the report, after providing adequate notice. Third, before the states begin to administer the block grants, they must certify to the relevant federal agency that they are prepared for administrative responsibilities; until that time, the federal agencies will continue to administer the programs as categorical grants. Finally, the act requires financial and compliance audits every two years, based upon standards established by the Comptroller General of the United States.

In addition to the requirements that apply to all of the block grants, there are a number of restrictions and mandates that pertain only to individal block grants. For instance, states may not use more than 10 percent of the funds for administrative costs in the alcohol and drug abuse and mental health block grants; no funds for administrative costs in the primary care block grant; and no more than 20 percent for administrative costs in the Title I education block grant. The health service block grant dictates that federal funds be used to supplement rather than replace state, local, or other nonfederal funds. The primary care, the maternal and child health, and the education block grants all provide for a certain amount of matching funds and maintenance of effort from the states. The primary care health block grant, the social services block grant, and the home energy assistance block grant all prescribe that the state *legislature* must hold a public hearing on the use of the federal funds.

4

Evaluating Block Grants: The Previous Experience and Future Expectations

The Reagan administration defended the six block-grant proposals it presented to Congress on two broad grounds: They would achieve more service at less cost because of administrative efficiencies, and they would provide the vehicle for the political and constitutional goal of returning proper authority to state and local governments.

In arguing the case for projected administrative efficiencies before the House Subcommittee on Manpower and Housing, OMB Director Stockman stated: "The block grant approach is an integral part of the president's program to bring about the country's economic recovery. This funding mechanism will streamline program administration by eliminating burdensome, cumbersome, and costly procedures currently in place."[1]

In the same testimony, Stockman laid out the political and constitutional argument for the block grants:

> [Block grants] will return responsibility for determining program composition and service levels to the more appropriate state and local levels of government. . . . We are proposing to move beyond a strategy of incremental reform. . . . We are proposing to allow states and localities to respond to and be responsible for their own needs, rather than to improve nationwide priorities and operating methods defined in Washington. . . . State and local governments are not ministerial appendages of the Federal government; they are functioning governments and should be treated as such.

This chapter will examine the administrative arguments regarding block grants, and the fifth chapter will look at some of the political implications.

[1] David A. Stockman, OMB director, testimony before the House Subcommittee on Manpower and Housing, April 28, 1981.

Block-Grant Performance

In evaluating the administration's claims for its block-grant proposals' efficiency and effectiveness, one can turn to the experience of the five block-grant programs created since 1966 and to the research of organizations and individuals who have analyzed them separately and collectively.

Before reviewing these findings, however, one should heed two caveats. First, none of the five existing block-grant programs is a "pure" block grant; that is, either the origin or history of each has caused some deviation from the design characteristics of block grants, making cross-cutting evaluation difficult. For instance, the 1966 Partnership in Health program was systematically ignored by Congress in the years after its passage and was surrounded by an increasing number (twenty to date) of categorical programs that logically should have been folded into it. The Safe Streets block grant became increasingly "categorized" during successive authorization proceedings. CETA was a hybrid from the outset—that is, it consisted of a combination of a block grant and a group of categorical programs within the same act.

Second, some of the data needed to construct cost estimates for the administration of federal grant programs either do not exist or have not been collected. In addition, there are major difficulties in interpreting the data where they do exist. For instance, the dividing line between administrative jobs and activities and operational jobs and activities is almost impossible to draw even by state or local governments with the best of wills, and often it is to state and local governments' advantage not to exercise the best of wills but to inflate or deflate their administrative costs. The situation is best summed up by the title of a recent General Accounting Office (GAO) study: "The Federal Government Should But Doesn't Know the Cost of Administering Its Assistance Programs."[2]

Both the GAO and the ACIR, which have extensively studied the operations of existing block grants, have offered general conclusions regarding this form of grant that are relevant to the administration's proposals.

On March 3, in hearings on the fiscal 1982 budget, Comptroller General Elmer Staats stated:

> The key to significantly improving the administration of federal domestic programs lies in the legislative consolidation of separate categorical programs serving similar objec-

[2] U. S., General Accounting Office (GAO), *The Federal Government Should But Doesn't Know the Cost of Administering Its Assistance Programs* (Washington, D.C., 1978).

tives into broader categories of assistance and the placing of like programs in a single agency. Accordingly, we strongly endorse the administration's consolidation initiative recognizing that the specific details are not yet available.[3]

A month later, after more details were available, the director of the GAO's Human Resources Division reaffirmed the strong endorsement of the block-grant proposals, but suggested certain changes, including reshuffling some individual programs among the consolidated grants; separating out maternal and child health programs and mental health and alcohol and drug abuse programs; revising the formula for the grants; allowing a longer transition and startup time for the states; establishing a uniform definition for low-income persons across the grants; and providing for greater accountability.[4]

ACIR, after a detailed examination of four existing block grants, concluded:

> The implementation record is mixed with respect to attainment of the management aims of the block grant. In general, however, experience under the four programs examined indicated that significant policy and administrative decentralization was achieved, federal personnel and paperwork costs were reduced, processes for facilitating interfunctional and intergovernmental coordination were established, and elected chief executives and legislators as well as administrative generalists were given significant roles in block grant decisionmaking. At the same time, recategorization and relatively low appropriation levels often limited the impact of these improvements and sometimes worked at cross purposes with the nature and intent of the instrument.[5]

[3] Elmer Staats, comptroller general, testimony before the House Committee on the Budget, March 3, 1981. GAO has called for major changes in the federal aid system for a number of years—including, particularly, grant consolidations; see, for instance, GAO, *Fundamental Changes are Needed in Federal Assistance to State and Local Governments* (Washington, D.C., 1975).

[4] Gregory J. Ahart, GAO director of Human Resources Division, testimony before the Senate Committee on Labor and Human Resources, April 2, 1981.

[5] ACIR, *Block Grants: A Comparative Analysis* (Washington, D.C., 1977), p. 39. The Congressional Budget Office (CBO) has not undertaken a detailed study of the impact of the current block-grant proposals, but CBO has expressed doubts about the administration's cost savings claims in a brief memorandum for Congress. See CBO, "Effects of Grant Consolidation in Education, Health, and Social Services on Administrative Costs" (Washington, D.C., May 1, 1981), unprocessed.
The memorandum states:

> The administration has argued that consolidation would produce sizeable offsetting savings. While there might be offsetting savings, any such . . . offsets are likely to fall far short of the proposed cuts. Indeed, there is some reason to expect that consolidation might even increase administrative costs and inefficiency, particularly in the short term. The available data, however, do

The mixed results that ACIR found in the block-grant administrative experience represent a pattern that is reflected throughout most of the research findings by individual scholars and research organizations.

The conclusions regarding three specific questions relevant to the claims about block grants illustrate this mixed pattern. The questions are the following.

1. Have the block grants produced a more efficient delivery of services that will resulc in reduced costs?

2. Have decentralization and local control resulted in more effective planning and coordination?

3. Have generalists (local and state elected officials and administrative generalists), who are more accountable to the electorate, assumed more control and direction of the programs?

Efficiency. In 1977 the GAO completed the study noted above, which constitutes the most extensive analysis to date on the costs of administering federal assistance programs. The study examined seventy-two grant programs, two of which were block-grant programs and the rest categorical programs.

Regarding its own conclusions as well as the conclusions of other studies, GAO cautioned at the outset that "attempts to analyze and compare the efficiency of the various administrative methods used have had limited success." It went on to state: "This is attributable in large part to the lack of systems that report information on financial and staff resources used in administering individual Federal assistance programs."[6]

Within the confines of these data limitations, GAO estimated that administrative costs among the seventy-two programs varied widely—from 0.3 percent to 28.5 percent. Regarding the comparative efficiency of the two block grants versus the seventy categorical grants, GAO found

> On the average, the two block grant programs we studied, CETA and LEAA [Law Enforcement Assistance Administration], had a higher administrative cost percentage and used more staff per $1 million of program funds than did

---

not permit a precise estimate of the change in costs. Moreover, the effects of consolidation are likely to vary among the proposed block grants because of differences among the services involved and among the current programs through which they are delivered.

[6] GAO, *The Federal Government Should But Doesn't Know the Costs of Administering Its Assistance Programs*, p. i.

categorical grant programs. Of the 70 categorical grant programs in our sample, 55 cost proportionately less to administer than did either of the block grant programs.[7]

GAO also noted, however, that a methodological flaw in its study probably caused an understatement of the administrative savings in block grants. Because it had been unable to define what constituted administrative costs at the project site (local) level, these costs were excluded from the calculations. GAO cited the experience of community development block grants to illustrate that many administrative savings from block grants might accrue at the last level of delivery. A 1976 Housing and Urban Development (HUD) report, GAO pointed out, had shown that under community development block grants, grant regulations had been reduced from 2,600 pages to 120 pages, the number of annual applications from 5 to 1, and the average application size from 1,400 pages to 40 or 50 pages. As GAO stated finally: "This indicates that the higher administrative costs above the [local] level may be offset by lower administrative costs at the [local] level."[8]

The complexities of interpreting the impact of block grants on red tape, administrative detail, and paperwork are further illustrated by the findings reported by the Brookings Institution evaluation of the workings of community development block grants.[9] The Brookings team reported that only twenty-one of forty-three mayors reported a decrease in red tape, with the remaining twenty-four reporting either no change or an increase. When one looks beneath those figures, however, one finds much of that discontent stemming from two sources: the imposition of a wholly new federal requirement internal to the program, Housing Assistance Plans; and crosscutting national requirements—such as environmental impact statements and equal opportunity issues—which during the 1970s began to have a major impact on all federal grants. Thus, the real complaints stemmed in large measure not from the consolidation of the eight categoricals into one program but from the additional requirements with which Congress freighted that change.

In a study, completed in April 1980, of eleven elementary- and secondary-education categorical programs administered by the Office of Education, GAO concluded that the amount of duplication of service among them was minimal and that consolidation would probably not produce significant administrative cost savings.

[7] Ibid., p. 16.
[8] Ibid., p. 17.
[9] Richard P. Nathan and Paul R. Dommel, "Federal-Local Relations under Block Grants," *Political Science Quarterly* (Fall 1978), pp. 428–29.

In the same report, however, GAO reverted to a theme in its earlier large-scale study of seventy-two federal aid programs—that essential data for detailed conclusions were not available.

> The fact that [federal, state and local] agencies have to deal with separate programs having different regulations and requirements as well as separate applications, separate evaluations and separate parent advisory councils, has undoubtedly created more administrative work and increased costs. But, because of differences in programs and variations in how State Education Agencies and Local Education Agencies are organized to administer them, determining how much additional burden is added by the numerous programs or the potential savings in administrative costs that would result from consolidation is difficult, if not impossible. . . . Office of Education officials could neither tell us how much their administrative costs were increased by the many Federal programs nor could they determine how much these costs could be reduced through consolidation. Without this information, the possible benefits of consolidation cannot be weighed against possible risks.[10]

Though often there are complicating external factors behind administrative deficiencies in the existing block grants, there are also instances simply of poor internal management. For example, GAO recently has found great laxness in state contracting practices in the existing social services block grant (Title XX) and has recommended that the Department of Health and Human Services strengthen its regulations regarding these procedures. And, in a report issued in April 1981, GAO took a number of cities to task for inadequate administrative practices in dispensing community development funds, particularly with regard to money going into housing rehabilitation.[11]

Decentralization, Planning, and Coordination. As noted above, ACIR in its analysis of the experience of four existing block grants, found that, in general, significant policy and administrative decentralization had taken place and intergovernmental and interfunctional coordination had been facilitated, but that recategorization and low funding levels had limited the impact of these and other program improvements.

Probably the most successful example of decentralization of de-

---

[10] GAO, *An Analysis of Concerns in Federal Educational Programs: Duplication of Services and Administrative Costs* (Washington, D.C., 1980), p. 25.

[11] GAO, *Federal and State Actions Needed to Overcome Problems in Administering the Title XX Programs* (Washington, D.C., 1980), and *The Community Development Block Grant Program Can Be More Effective in Revitalizing the Nation's Cities* (Washington, D.C., 1981).

cisionmaking occurred in the community development block grant. As the Brookings Institution evaluation noted: "The CDBG program has resulted in the decentralization of decisionmaking authority from the federal to the local level, compared with the older-style HUD categorical aid program." Thirty-eight of the forty-four cities in the Brookings survey reported a reduced HUD role.[12] During the Carter administration, HUD officials moved by means of additional regulations to reestablish some control over funding activities and priorities, but even with those changes, local officials retained and exercised a great degree of discretion. In addition, about 53 percent of the block-grant money went for new spending programs, as opposed to maintaining programs that had been funded under the categorical programs—a strong indication that local officials were exercising independent judgment on priorities.[13]

The Safe Streets block grant was also effective as a decentralizing device. The program covered a broad range of law enforcement activities, and states were given adequate authority to identify their own problems and create programs to deal with them. ACIR's analysis shows that a coordinated process for efforts to reduce crime was established and funds were targeted generally to jurisdictions having the most serious needs. On the negative side, however, the State Planning Agencies which run the programs never became part of most of the state and local criminal justice systems. And Congress almost every year added new earmarked categories to the grant and thus constricted discretion.[14]

The social services (Title XX) block grant is the newest of the block grants, going back only to late 1975. Separate studies completed in 1978 by the National Governors Association and the Urban Institute concluded that the goals of comprehensive planning and coordination in the social service area had not materialized by that time. The Governors Association study also suggested that part of the problem was the lack of internal program evaluation and assessment of the needs of the service populations. The Urban Institute study, however, found that, despite severe funding restrictions, there was already evidence that the states were exercising independent judgment and changing the allocation of resources. While the data were "fragmentary," stated the Urban Institute report, they did suggest

[12] Richard P. Nathan and Paul R. Dommel, "Federal-Local Relations under Block Grants," pp. 425–26, 442.
[13] Rudolph G. Penner, "Reforming the Grants System," in Peter Mieskowski and William E. Oakland, eds., *Fiscal Federalism and Grants-in-Aid* (Washington, D.C.: Urban Institute, 1979), p. 129.
[14] ACIR, *Block Grants: A Comparative Analysis*, pp. 18–28.

"major shifts which may have stemmed from the Title XX experience."[15]

Generalist Control. Closely related to decentralization is the issue of whether or not generalists (local elected officials such as the mayor and city council and top administrators such as city managers) have assumed control or whether the specialists (appointees to special districts, functional specialists, and others) associated with categorical programs still pull the levers.

Here again, as in the area of decentralization, the community development block grant achieved the greatest success, both in statutory underpinning and in subsequent actual practice. The eligibility provisions of the authorizing act clearly favored local, elected officials in general units of government—cities over 50,000 population in standard metropolitan statistical areas and urban counties over 200,000. Also, the Brookings evaluation found that local government officials, particularly chief executives, did play a more influential role than they had under the prior categorical programs. The study noted:

> Local chief executives and other generalist officials of the executive have been the principal actors. This applies both to the procedural and substantive aspects of the CDBG [Community Development Block Grants] program. There was significant involvement by local legislatures in nearly half of the sample units in the first year of the CDBG program.[16]

Both the Safe Streets and the Partnership for Health block grants achieved a fair degree of generalists' participation and control, but both also illustrated the difficulties of achieving a true integration in the state and local political systems. In the case of the Partnership for Health grant, a low level of funding and the continual addition of categorical grants in the same functional area undercut any possibility that it would play a significant role in state health planning and operations. It became in time a gap filler, a fund that state officials could use to make up deficiencies in the health area.[17]

---

[15] Peter S. O'Donnell, *Social Services: Three Years after Title XX* (Washington, D.C.: National Governors Association, Center for Policy Research, 1978) *passim*; Bill Benton, Tracy Field, and Rhona Miller, *Social Services Federal Legislation vs. State Implementation* (Washington, D.C.: Urban Institute, 1978), pp. 9–12, 113.

[16] Richard P. Nathan and Paul R. Dommel, "Monitoring the Block Grant Program for Community Development," *Political Science Quarterly* (Summer 1977), p. 231.

[17] ACIR, *Block Grants: A Comparative Analysis*, p. 18; see also Leonard Robbins, "The Impact of Converting Categorical into Block Grants: The Lessons from the 314(d) Block Grants in the Partnership for Health Act," *Publius: The Journal of Federalism* (Winter 1976), pp. 50–70.

A low funding level also limited the involvement of generalists in the Safe Streets grant. The program usually became identified with, and controlled by, the governor's office (the governor usually established and named the members of the State Planning Agency mandated under the grant). Further, in some states governors actively resisted efforts by the state legislatures to use the program. Thus, it was difficult in many states to tie these federal anticrime funds to state outlays or to integrate this program with broader state legislative efforts in the criminal justice area.[18]

Carl W. Stenberg of the ACIR staff has posited general conditions for generalists' participation and non-participation in block grants, under the title "The Myth of the Generalist":

> According to this "myth," the generalist has the interest, commitment, and capacity to make all decisions relating to the block grant. Yet realistically, where the generalist is a part-time official, the aided function is not a traditional activity or one that is heavily supported by direct revenue, the program area is technical or complex or the amount of federal funding is small, these officials have not become the key actors in the decisionmaking process. In these cases, specialists may continue to be highly influential, as generalists will be unwilling or unable to keep on top of developments.
>
> On the other hand, where a federally aided area is visible, controversial, and politically sensitive, generalists will probably attempt to play a major role even when some of the foregoing conditions are present. This has been evident in the crime control, manpower and community development programs. The basic point here is that unlike many categoricals, block grants give generalists the *opportunity* [italics added] to become involved in decisionmaking.[19]

The Reagan Proposals and Lessons from the Block-Grant Experience

While there are important differences in the individual histories of the existing block grants, there are also certain lessons that can be drawn. One fact particularly stands out: In most cases external conditions and factors were more important in determining how a block grant worked than the particular administrative capabilities of local and state governments. Thus, the level of funding that a block grant achieved, the amount of recategorization Congress imposed over the

[18] Ibid, pp. 27–28.
[19] Carl W. Stenberg, "The Federal Grant Maze," p. 11.

years, and the attitude and performance of the executive agency in charge of the grant constituted the most important variables affecting block-grant performance. It is probably no great exaggeration to state, then, that after Reagan block grants pass, the most important key to their success will be the existence through the rest of the decade of benign, supportive presidential administrations, combined with Congresses that exercise restraint in relation to changing the ground rules and recategorizing the programs.

A second lesson from the history of block grants relevant to the current proposals is the danger of overexpectation. For instance, the LEAA grants never amounted to more than 5 percent of a state's criminal justice budget, and the Partnership in Health grants did not account for more than 3 percent of reported state health department expenditures in the same areas.[20] Thus, it was just not possible for them to attain the leverage to produce major changes in the way states and localities planned or administered their programs in these areas.

The Reagan block grants were coupled with an initial 25 percent reduction in existing programs and with further cuts that might have resulted in 60 percent reductions in 1985. As in the cases of the LEAA and Partnership in Health, however, these new consolidated grants might lead to reductions in red tape and in administrative costs, but not—as was hoped from earlier block grants—to major shifts in a state's total social or health program priorities or to great innovations in service delivery. They are not likely, in and of themselves, to have that much leverage and influence.

Finally, will new block grants lead to greater control by elected officials and top bureaucratic generalists? Stenberg's conclusions about existing block grants remain relevant for the future. As in the past, there will be conditions and circumstances that will work for and against generalist control, but block grants, unlike categorical grants, will give generalists the *opportunity* to exercise control if they so choose.

Model Legislation

As pointed out previously, the Reagan proposals, though labeled block grants, in many ways resembled more closely President Nixon's special revenue-sharing proposals. There were no matching or maintenance of effort requirements, for instance, and program guidelines and provisions for accountability—purposes, plans, audits, public

[20] Ad Hoc Coalition on Block Grants, "Block Grant Briefing Book," mimeographed (Washington, D.C., 1981), pp. II 6, II 15.

participation, and recipient eligibility—were kept to a bare minimum.

Given what is known regarding the history of existing block grants, problems are likely to arise from the looseness of the administrative requirements and the vagueness of congressional instructions and mandates, both to federal executive agencies and to the state and local governments. To circumvent this result, a number of provisions should be included in the legislation authorizing block grants to clarify the purposes of the acts and to tighten administrative procedures, without greatly reducing flexibility for the state and local governments.

Specifically, Congress and the administration should consider the following provisions as models for future block-grant legislation.

1. *Purposes.* The statements of purpose in the Reagan administration's six block-grant proposals were couched in vague, general language. The activities included were listed, but the intended goals were not. To the extent possible the statement of purpose should lay out the intended goals for each of the general activities; for instance, reduction of infant mortality or reduction of the incidence of disease among migrants. Positing a goal will give the state clearer direction and allow more accurate evaluation later.

2. *Reports and public participation.* The Reagan legislation required states to prepare and make available for public comment, prior to the expenditure of block-grant funds, reports on their intended use; but there was no requirement for public hearings. Because many public and special interest groups fear that the states will ignore their interests, the public participation provisions should be tightened. One approach would be to allow the states either to hold a separate public hearing or to integrate the block grant into their normal budgetary and legislative processes. If, for instance, the state legislatures reappropriated the funds, then the appropriations hearings could be used as a forum for debate on their allocation. (Congress added a public hearing requirement to the Reagan block-grant legislation.)

3. *Audits.* The Reagan proposals provided for an independent audit every two years but did not lay down guidelines for the nature or contents of the audit. In order to ensure uniform data and evaluation, Congress should make the audits conform to some existing standards—such as the OMB circulars or the GAO's Standards for Audit of Governmental Organizations, Programs, Activities, and Functions. (Congress provided for use of the GAO standards for auditing money spent under the block grants.)

4. *Administrative costs limit.* Local government representatives have expressed strong concern that state bureaucracies will eat up a dis-

proportionate share of already limited funds in administrative costs. As noted in this chapter, great difficulties exist in defining such costs. But Congress should consider placing a limit for each block grant on the total percentage that could go for overhead. This limitation would allow flexibility for disparate administrative costs from the individual categorical grants being folded in, but at the same time it would serve as a caution to the states that they would be watched for costly, inefficient administration. (Congress placed administrative cost limits on some, but not all, of the Reagan block-grant proposals.)

5. *Effective date.* The Reagan block-grant legislation had an effective date of October 1, 1981. This provision should have been changed to allow implementation for a period of up to two years. In the future, when the changes contemplated in block-grant legislation necessitate changes in state laws or constitute new state responsibilities, the states should be given time to plan for the transition, to restructure their executive departments, and otherwise to integrate these new responsibilities into their own budgeting and legislative processes. (Congress provided for a transition period for the Reagan block grants.)

6. *Eligibility.* The categorical grants that were repealed contained a bewildering array of eligibility requirements. The original block-grant legislation (with the exception of the local education grant, which was limited to handicapped and educationally disadvantaged students and students in schools undergoing desegregation) allowed the states to establish their own eligibility requirements. State flexibility on this issue must be improved; but, at the same time, clearly the programs being folded into the block grants are aimed particularly at poor people. Therefore, it would make sense—and would clear up much confusion that exists in the present system—for Congress at least to specify a uniform definition of low income persons.

5

The Political Dimensions of the Reagan Block-Grant Proposals

In addition to raising questions relating to the effectiveness and efficiency of program delivery and to the roles of the three federal partners, the Reagan administration proposals—and the clear political purposes behind them—have also touched off a straightforward struggle for political power and access. The block-grant legislation directly challenges many of the alliances, interrelationships, and working arrangements that have evolved over the past two decades in and around the federal intergovernmental aid system.

In brief, the chief results of the Reagan block-grant proposals, coupled with the administration's future intentions, will be

- a greatly enhanced role for state governments
- major reduction in the direct ties between local governments and the federal government
- an uncertain and hazardous future for the community-action and nonprofit organizations, which have served as quasi-public entities at the local level, dispensing social services largely with federal dollars
- a fifty-state "free-for-all" competition for block-grant funds among interest groups currently served by the social services, education, and health categorical grants

Whatever the outcome of the struggle, the alertness and political muscle of groups with a vested interest in existing arrangements have been amply demonstrated over the past few months. Within weeks after the administration unveiled its plans to revamp the federal grant system and to withdraw gradually from a number of areas, a coalition of over sixty organizations was put together to fight the proposals. The membership of the group, the Ad Hoc Coalition on Block Grants, is a composite of the organizations whose position within the current system may well be threatened and of representatives of special interest groups who have a direct stake in particular categorical programs. There are representatives of community-action organizations, who under many categorical programs have constituted the outposts of the federal delivery system: the Housing Assistance Council, the National Association of Community Based Organizations, and the National Council of Community Mental Health Centers, for instance. There are representatives of particular subcategories of the populations who have benefited from individual program grants: education (the National Education Association and the National Retired Teachers Association); the elderly (the American Association of Retired Persons and the Gray Panthers); children (the Children's Defense Fund and the Children's Foundation); the handicapped (the American Association for Retarded Citizens and the Information Center for Handicapped Individuals); minorities (the National Urban League, the National Council of La Raza, and the National Hispanic Housing Coalition); rural interests (Rural America, the Rural Housing Coalition, and the Rural Coalition); and neighborhoods (the National Association of Neighborhoods, the National Congress for Community Economic Development, and the Neighborhood Coalition). In addition there are national organizations such as the League of Women Voters and the United Automobile Workers who on more general grounds oppose not only the movement toward block grants but also the shifting of domestic priorities that go with the change.

The Ad Hoc Coalition lobbied Congress intensely, and with some success, against the Reagan block-grant proposals. Composed of organizations and individuals who are intimately familiar with the workings of the federal grant system, it put forward comprehensive and, in some instances, telling analyses of the administrative weaknesses of some block grants and well-documented defenses of some existing categorical programs.[1]

Interestingly, though the administration and its opponents disagree on the administrative and program-delivery vices and virtues of categorical and block grants, they are in substantial agreement about the dimensions of the political contest. The most important political questions, both sides agree, revolve around the administration's determination to force not only program authority but also political decision making, with all the struggle that entails, down to the state level. As noted earlier, administration spokesmen readily state that they are out to break up the iron triangles in Washington. Henceforth, local governments and constituency groups should look to the state capitols and not to the federal government. Washington-based national organizations, they assert, would be well advised to

[1] Ad Hoc Coalition on Block Grants, "Block Grants Briefing Book," mimeographed (Washington, D.C., 1981), pp. I 5, II 1–24, III 1–27.

strengthen their staffs at the fifty state capitals around the country. State and local governments, they contend, are closer to the voters and more responsive to their needs.

The Ad Hoc Coalition sees the consequences of the devolution of power quite differently. It states that the block-grant proposals will result in a "brutal political struggle at the state level where the poor and others without clout will often be the losers." Further, it argues that another

> consequence of the block grants will be to pit disadvantaged communities against one another in conflicts over a smaller pie. The handicapped will be pitted against the aged, foster care parents against child care advocates, and black lung victims against mental health patients. The block grant will politicize and brutalize the allocation of scarce dollars far more than does the current system.[2]

The remainder of this chapter will explore the most important political consequences of the proposed devolution of power to the states. It will attempt to answer three questions. First, what is the situation today regarding state government, and will the changes contemplated at the federal level have any impact on the relations and balance of power between the governors and the state legislatures? Second, what are some of the likely results for the other major deliverers of service—local governments and community-based and nonprofit organizations? Finally, what will happen to the interest groups that are the recipients of the social, education, and health programs being proposed for block grants?

State Governments

Over the last two decades, the situation with regard to state governments has changed greatly. The Supreme Court's one man–one vote decision, the ensuing reapportionment, and constitutional modernization have all combined to alter substantially the way state governments do business and deal with the problems of their constituencies.

The power of most governors has been strengthened through the increase in the number of appointed officials, the acquisition of the authority to reorganize state executive departments, and the creation of a formal executive budget process. In addition, most governors now serve a four-year term and are eligible for reelection.

Besides becoming more representative, state legislatures have emerged as much more effective lawmaking bodies. Over thirty state legislatures now meet annually. Salaries of lawmakers have been raised, and professional staff support has been increased. Internally,

[2] Ibid., pp. I 6, V 16.

the state legislatures have increased their oversight function, streamlined the legislative process, and reorganized their committee structures.

One important trend in state legislatures will have a direct impact on federal grants and on the legislatures' relationship with the governors in exercising control over those grants. Twelve states now provide for a formal reappropriation of all federal funds that come into the states. Over thirty other states have enacted some kind of less formal control, but it is likely that in the near future—particularly if the administration's block-grant proposals pass—a number of them will also move to fold federal money directly into the state appropriations process. The assertion of the authority of the state legislature in this area will in turn change the relationship between the federal government and the governors, who in the past, more because of convenience and happenstance than because of planning or collusion, have been the chief, and often sole, point of contact between the federal agencies administering grants and the state.

State revenue systems have also been made more efficient and progressive. By 1979, forty-one states had enacted an income tax; forty-five, a corporate income levy; and the same number a general sales tax. Thirty-seven states used a combination of all three of these revenue sources in 1979, whereas only nineteen did in 1960. Much of this new revenue has gone into social programs to help the poor, into education, into health care and hospitals, and into local transportation systems. A number of states now have their own form of revenue sharing with local governments. (See figure 1 for illustrations of changes in state machinery of government.)[3]

Not all is perfect by any means. The GAO in recent years has, on occasion, severely criticized state agencies for inadequate planning, procurement policy, and overall administration of federal grant money and programs. And an ACIR study recently concluded that only a few states had developed "broad and comprehensive strategies which can bring state assistance to bear on community problems in coordinated fashion."[4]

Many mayors, particularly mayors of big cities, remain skeptical of the ability of many state governments to handle the increased responsibilities contemplated by the Reagan administration. Mayor

[3] Carl W. Stenberg, "Federalism in Transition: 1959–1979," *Intergovernmental Perspective* (Winter 1980), pp. 9–10; David B. Walker,"The States and the System: Changes and Choices," *Intergovernmental Perspective* (Fall 1980), pp. 6–12.

[4] ACIR, *The States and Distressed Communities* (Washington, D.C., 1981), p. 58; see also Charles R. Warren, *The States and Urban Strategies: A Comparative Analysis* (Washington, D.C.: The National Academy of Public Administration, 1980).

FIGURE 1
Changes in State Government, 1960–1978

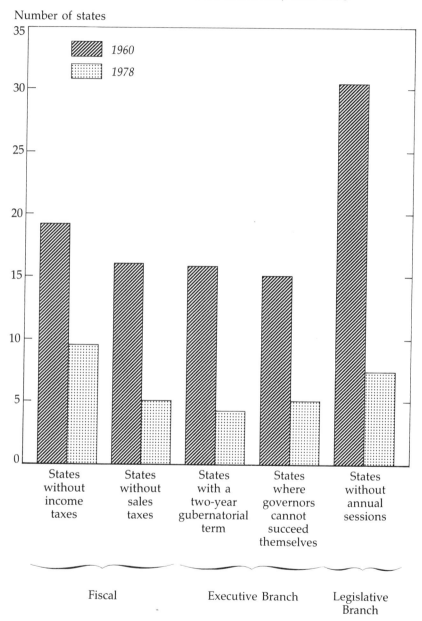

SOURCE: Council of State Governments and the American Petroleum Institute.

Maynard Jackson of Atlanta asserted at the U.S. Conference of Mayors convention in June 1981 that only four of the fifty states would do an adequate job under the block grants. Mayor Charles Royer of Seattle has also questioned whether the states are "ready for the political and fiscal hand grenade being tossed them by the President."[5]

Governors and representatives from state legislatures, though quite worried by the budget cuts that go with the block grants and the speed with which the administration wants to implement the legislation, argue strongly that most states are ready to accept the new responsibilities. Replying to the criticism expressed by some mayors, Governor Richard Thornburg of Pennsylvania has stated that they are "a bum rap for the states—an unfair resurrection of shopworn arguments that the states are incompetent or insensitive to the needs of the poor."[6]

Any system with fifty components is bound to produce mixed results. Certainly many of the states today have the potential institutional and administrative ability to handle their new responsibilities. But whether or not the political processes within them are open and responsive enough to encompass and accommodate the interests of the groups now dependent on the categorical programs remains an open question.

Not surprisingly given the central elements of Reagan federalism, the nation's governors and state legislatures are among the strongest supporters of the block grants. Representatives of the National Governors Association and the National Conference of State Legislatures have assiduously lobbied Hill committees in favor of the legislation. Scott Bunton of the National Governors Association staff stated, "Basically the governors feel—and they have argued this on the Hill—that if they're going to have to absorb a 25 percent reduction in funds, they've got to have some relief from all the red tape and administrative complexity that go with categorical programs. The worst of all possible worlds would be to get the budget cuts and no program consolidations."[7]

Local Governments: Cities and Counties

Reagan administration officials see a significant diminution in the direct ties that have grown up between the federal government and

[5] Charles Royer, quoted in Neil R. Peirce, "The Right Thing in the Wrong Way," *Baltimore Sun*, May 25, 1981.

[6] Richard Thornburg, quoted ibid.

[7] Interview by the author with Scott Bunton, staff member of the National Governors Association, April 20, 1981.

local governments. Cities and counties, in the view of the administration, are the creatures of the state governments and not of the federal government. Thus, though they provide for direct pass-through of funds in a few cases, the president's block grants place most allocation decisions in the hands of state officials.

Local government organizations are divided in their reactions to the administration's proposals: the National Association of Counties (NACo) has generally been supportive; the National League of Cities, though opposed to some parts of the Reagan proposals, has not actively lobbied against those proposals; but the United States Conference of Mayors has taken an increasingly hostile position.

Though it has certain specific changes it would like to see made in the administration's block-grant bills—for instance, provision for direct pass-through of money for traditionally local services, a cap on state administrative expenses, and involvement of local officials in development of state plans—NACo has adhered to its long-established position in favor of grant consolidation. A NACo official, testifying before the Senate Subcommittee on Intergovernmental Affairs, stated:

> We in county government recognize the great need to consolidate nearly 500 active federal grant programs. Consolidation has been the keystone of NACo's policy on grant reform for nearly a decade. I do not believe I need to argue the benefits consolidation offers. . . . They are a matter of record. It is becoming abundantly clear that consolidation is no longer a luxury, but rather a necessity of our times.[8]

NACo officials are aware, however, of the administration's announced intentions of phasing the federal government out of many of the programs included in the block grants. For this reason, in sessions with White House officials, NACo representatives have pressed hard for the administration to proceed quickly with plans for a second goal: the turnback of federal taxing resources to the states and local governments. Stated Bruce Talley of the NACo staff:

> On at least three occasions, the president has stated his intention to move forward with the tax turnbacks plan and county officials strongly feel that the administration should not put this on a back burner. It is the second part of a two-way compact between the administration and state and local governments: Along with budget cuts must go adequate

[8] Conrad Joyner, supervisor, Pima County, Arizona, testimony before Senate Subcommittee on Intergovernmental Relations, March 11, 1981.

resources to state and local governments to allow them to pick up the programs the federal government is dropping.[9]

The opposition of the Conference of Mayors stems, to a large degree, from reaction to the Reagan budget cuts, which mayors of large cities (who tend to dominate the conference) argue fall disproportionately on urban areas. But the opposition also evolves from a strong sense that under the Reagan presidency and Reagan new federalism, the power and influence of cities—particularly the big cities—will be reduced. As one Washington staff official said: "They are waking up to the fact that they're a long way from the days when Jack Watson [assistant to the president for intergovernmental affairs under President Carter] was on constant alert to hold their hands."

The mayors have several concerns about block grants: that the grants will just exchange one bureaucracy (federal) for another (state); that a great deal of money will be eaten up by state administrative costs; that many state legislatures will not be responsive to urban needs; and that mayors will have little say in the development of state plans to allocate the money.

The mayors refused to give outright endorsement to the Reagan administration block-grant proposals at their annual conference in June, despite a long history of favoring these changes in their federal aid system. Probably in the future both sides will move to "mend fences"; the Reagan White House is not likely, however, to change its course of lodging power and responsibility with state governments rather than with local governments.

Community-Action and Nonprofit Organizations

The Great Society legislation of the 1960s produced several thousand local community-action and nonprofit organizations which have acted in many instances as delivery agents for government services to the poor.

There are over 850 local Community Action Agencies (CAAs) that were created originally under the Economic Opportunity Act of 1964 and today operate through the Community Services Administration. Two-thirds of the CAAs operate as private nonprofit organizations, with control vested in a board composed of local officials, businessmen, and representatives of the poor. CAAs are located in over 2,000 counties, cities, and towns. They are funded largely through federal dollars in the delivery of various services, including health care, food and nutrition, education, job training, weatherization,

[9] Interview by the author with Bruce Talley, staff member of the National Association of Counties, April 22, 1981.

housing assistance, rural transportation, senior-citizen services, and Head Start centers.

In addition to the CAAs, numerous other community-based and nonprofit organizations—rural groups, neighborhood groups, church-related organizations, and others—serve as delivery agents for federal, state, and local services.

All of these groups are doubly hit by the proposals of the Reagan administration. First, though many of them received some funds from local and state governments, their main fiscal lifeline has been federal dollars. The Reagan budget cuts in the social, health, and eduation areas are likely to reduce their activities drastically. Second, the proposed move to block grants will force these groups to compete and lobby for funds at the state and local levels. In contrast to the current situation where they often look to federal agencies for project grants for specific purposes, they will have to compete in the future for an open-ended and smaller pot of money to be dispensed by the state legislatures, county commissioners, and city councils.

The Ad Hoc Coalition on Block Grants has projected the following results if the budget cuts and the block-grant proposals are enacted:

> The federal cuts associated with the block grants will be replicated for most service providers at the local level. Many private agencies that are heavily dependent on federal funds, such as community action agencies, community health centers, day care programs and rehabilitation facilities, may be forced to close. Pressure will develop about who should be served. As resources vanish and federal eligibility requirements are abolished, local service delivery agencies will be forced to make more decisions, based on their own criteria about who gets served. Within the tight budget environment that will exist, these decisions will be subject to intense scrutiny and criticism.[10]

The Reagan administration acknowledges that its proposals will mean increased competition for fewer dollars by the community-based and nonprofit organizations and more difficult resource-allocation choices, but it argues that the process is healthy and necessary. OMB Director Stockman, appearing before the House Subcommittee on Manpower and Housing, was closely questioned about the fate of CAAs under the administration's proposals. Stockman stated that undoubtedly some of the CAAs would not survive. The test, he said, was whether or not they were "providing services on a cost-effective basis." This

[10] Ad Hoc Coalition on Block Grants, "Block Grant Briefing Book," p. IV 9.

was not a "harmful" or "deleterious" result, he argued, but part of a "necessary winnowing out process." No government or private organization, he concluded, should be "thought of [as existing] in perpetuity."[11]

In summary, the network of social service organizations which have acted as surrogates for the government over the past decade faces an uncertain future, and the winnowing process described by OMB Director Stockman will likely result in a much smaller number of these organizations in the coming years.

Special Interest Groups

As one observer has commented, should the Reagan proposals go through, the representatives of the poor and disadvantaged face a "wrenching readjustment" as they move from the "wholesale" form of lobbying in Washington to "retailing their point of view in fifty state capitals."[12]

As noted above, opponents of the Reagan administration proposals foresee a "brutal political struggle" at the state level which will pit one group against another—handicapped against aged, child-care advocates against foster-care parents, and black-lung victims against mental-health patients. Though administration spokesmen would no doubt disagree that the struggle will be necessarily "brutal," they have stated bluntly that their aim is to place these struggles, whether benign or brutal, at the state and local levels of government.

Political scientists have long noted the connection between the "nationalization of public policy" and the nationalization of pressure-group influence. As Deil S. Wright has suggested:

> To maximize their effectiveness, while minimizing costs (broadly defined), pressure groups have taken their causes (and their headquarters) to the nation's capital. From this vantage, they influence the initiation, enactment, and implementation of major public policies, including grant-in-aid programs.[13]

It is this connection between the nationalization of public policy and the nationalization of lobbying and political pressure that the Reagan administration avowedly wants to break. The president has spoken quite candidly about this goal. In a June meeting with Republican

[11] David A. Stockman, OMB director, testimony before the House Subcommittee on Manpower and Housing, April 28, 1981.
[12] Neal R. Peirce, "The Right Thing in the Wrong Way," *Baltimore Sun*, May 25, 1981.
[13] Deil S. Wright, *Federal Grants-in-Aid: Perspectives and Alternatives* (Washington, D.C.: American Enterprise Institute, 1968), p. 32.

members of the House Appropriations Committee regarding budget strategy, he is reported to have stated: "It's far easier for people to come to Washington to get their social programs. It would be a hell of a lot tougher if we diffuse them, and send them out to the states. All their friends and connections are in Washington."[14]

Commenting on the statement of the president and similar statements by other high ranking White House officials, Steven V. Roberts of the *New York Times* concluded:

> The stated purpose of [the] block grants is not just to improve efficiency, but to further conservative ideals. . . . The block grant strategy flows partly from a deeply-held Republican belief that Washington contains a powerful network of liberal power centers—lobbyists and bureaucrats, Congressional staff members, and national news reporters. Dispersing decisionmaking responsibility to the states, goes the argument, would undermine such forces, and thus changes the basic priorities of government.[15]

Should the Reagan administration succeed in moving a large number of categorical programs into block grants and devolving authority to the states, the political results in the fifty state capitals are impossible to predict in detail, because the political configurations of the affected interest groups and the balance of power among them would vary widely.

On one hand, groups that have strong state or local chapters would begin with some advantage. Thus Benjamin L. Hooks, the head of the National Association for the Advancement of Colored People, although he strongly opposes block grants, has recently expressed confidence that the 1800 local chapters would allow the organization to compete very effectively for support at both the local and state level. Other groups such as the Gray Panthers (elderly) and the National Education Association (teachers) are also highly organized across the country. Representatives of the handicapped—particularly of handicapped children—are thought to be in a strong position in most states; indeed, the handicapped are thought to be so strong that one of the arguments to keep their programs out of any block grants is that, as one Senate committee staff person said, "if they are thrown into competition with most of these other disadvantaged groups, they will sweep the field—take all the money."

On the other hand, the rural poor and migrant workers, lacking strong organizational bases, might very well fare poorly in many

[14] Quoted in Steven V. Roberts, "Budget Ax Becomes a Tool for Social Change," *New York Times,* June 21, 1981.
[15] Ibid.

states. And family planning advocates, because of the strong social and moral divisions that currently wrack the country regarding contraception and abortion, would face great difficulty in some states maintaining the level of support they now enjoy under the targeted federal categorical aid.

All of this, of course, is sheer speculation, and all that one can say with certainty is that, as one commentator stated, "It's going to be a 'grab-bag' situation for some time to come."[16]

Two other potential long-range results from a large-scale move from categorical programs to block grants should be noted. The first is the possible impact on congressional organization. There are now 147 subcommittees in the House and 90 in the Senate. This degree of specialization and fragmented power is tied directly to the federal grant-in-aid system and particularly to the hundreds of categorical programs in a variety of domestic policy areas. Over time, a move toward broader-based aid, giving more discretion to state and local governments and resting on enduring formulas, would undermine the power and influence of the subcommittees, particularly of the chairmen.

A similar phenomenon would likely occur in the executive departments and agencies. Offices and bureaus which have as their main work the detailed policing of categorical programs could, over time, be consolidated, with a concomitant reduction in the number of civil servants needed to monitor the federal grant-in-aid system.

All in all, while many political consequences of the Reagan administration proposals remain uncertain, they are likely to be substantial and far-reaching.

[16] Richard P. Nathan, lecture delivered at the National Health Policy Forum, Washington, D.C., May 19, 1981.

6
Federalism in the Eighties: Sorting Out Responsibilities

Preceding chapters have focused in some detail on the intricacies of the federal grant system and on the potential consequences of the Reagan administration's plans to consolidate over eighty categorical grant programs into six broadly structured block grants. But to remain bound by the dense thicket of the intergovernmental grant system would be to miss a much larger and more important set of issues. The thesis of this chapter, and, indeed, the ultimate point of this monograph, is that the Reagan administration has the opportunity to guide and shape a major reshuffling and redivision of responsibilities in the American federal system. If it succeeds, this sorting out of responsibilities can combine political benefits with the achievement of a sounder, more rational federal system.

The belief that the time is ripe for a more rational division of responsibilities among the federal, state, and local governments crosses party lines and includes among its proponents individuals and organizations along a wide band of the political spectrum. As early as 1975, David A. Stockman, in an article in *Public Interest,* called for a "fundamental shift in social policy strategy," that entailed the national government's establishing a "comprehensive national health insurance program and universal income maintenance," while at the same time ceasing to fund most other individual categorical social service programs (see appendix A). ACIR, working under the chairmanship of former New York City Mayor Abraham D. Beame and including among its members both Democras and Republicans, has called for the federal assumption of financial responsibility for employment security, housing assistance, medical benefits, and basic nutrition programs. In turn, ACIR recommends that the federal government should consolidate, phase-out, or terminate many of the remaining federal assistance programs. The National Governors Association and the National Conference of State Legislatures have suggested that, in exchange for federal takeover of welfare, the state and local governments should assume full responsibility for education, transportation, and law-enforcement programs. Using arguments quite similar to those of Reagan White House officials, Governor Bruce Babbitt, a liberal Democrat from Arizona, has taken the lead with concrete proposals for the governors and state legislators to negotiate with the Reagan administration.

Finally, a blue-ribbon presidential commission given the task of developing a national agenda for the next decade—the President's Commission for a National Agenda for the Eighties—concluded that the top priority on a social agenda should be the enactment of a competitive, market-oriented national health-insurance program and of a minimum-security income base for all citizens. Concomitantly, this group, which was appointed by President Carter and was composed of Democrats, Republicans, and independents, stated that "the federal government is overloaded" and that it should turn over to state and local governments responsibility for implementing many of the programs encompassed in the 600-odd narrow-purpose categorical aid programs.

As officials of the Reagan administration in its early months revealed their long-range plans—and the rationale behind them—for domestic policy, the profound implications of the contemplated changes became increasingly evident. Richard P. Nathan stated: "The Reagan program makes domestic and social policy changes of an historic character, although packaged . . . as economic policy. It represents the most radical shift in domestic policy since the New Deal."[1]

As Nathan, Senator Daniel Patrick Moynihan (Democrat, New York), and others have noted—and in Moynihan's case pugnaciously protested—the budget process is being used effectively by the Reagan administration not only to combat inflation but also to redirect federal policy. Should the president's new budget priorities prevail over the next four years, the federal government's support of social services would be drastically curtailed, while defense spending would rise substantially. It is estimated that under the administration's projected budgets, defense spending will rise 8 percent per year (in real dollars) and nondefense funding will decline about 15 percent over the next five years.[2]

A second radical shift in domestic policy relates to federalism and intergovernmental relations. Just as the current debate over the fiscal 1982 proposed budget cuts is only the first skirmish in a larger struggle to reshape national priorities, so, too, are the president's

[1] Richard P. Nathan, lecture delivered at the National Health Policy Forum, Washington, D.C., May 19, 1981.
[2] Congressional Budget Office, *An Analysis of President Reagan's Budget Revision for Fiscal Year 1982* (Washington, D.C., March 1981), p. xiv.

six block-grant proposals only the first step toward the larger goals of reshuffling the division of responsibilities between the federal and state governments and of simultaneously changing the political ground rules of the current division of responsibilities between the two levels of government.

The Administration's Announced Intentions

It could be argued that the administration is already well advanced toward reordering federal, state, and local responsibilities. Even without factoring in inflation, the 25 percent budget cuts proposed in the program areas of the six block grants will shift a substantial burden to states and localities. For the future, the administration intends to hold each of the block grants (except the local education grant) to the level of the fiscal 1982 budget through fiscal 1985. Using the inflation rates projected by the administration, it is estimated that holding these programs constant will result in an average reduction across all the block grants of almost 60 percent.[3]

Administration spokesmen have also been surprisingly candid about their ultimate plans for these program areas, even though the admission has played into the hands of opponents of the current block-grant legislation. For instance, White House Assistant Robert Carleson has publicly stated that the block grants are the first step toward total withdrawal of the federal government from the education, health, and social services programs that are therein encompassed. In an interview he added: "Most if not all of these programs are properly the responsibility of the states. Few would meet the burden of proof that they are truly national in scope and purpose." Carleson also argued that the return of responsibility and authority to the states is "even closer to Ronald Reagan's heart than the budget cuts. . . . The budget cuts became the first priority because of the economic situation we inherited, but the president has been calling for these changes in the federal system throughout his entire political career."[4]

In a number of meetings with state and local government officials, the president has referred to a "dream" that he has regarding the future of federalism:

[3] Jule M. Sugarman, "Human Services in the 1980s: A White Paper for Citizens and Government Officials," pp. 16–20.
[4] Interview by the author with Robert B. Carleson, special assistant to the President for Human Resources, May 19, 1981. Also Robert B. Carleson, lecture delivered at the National Health Policy Forum, Washington, D.C., June 2, 1981.

I have a dream of my own. I think block grants are only the intermediate step. I dream of the day when the federal government can substitute for [block grants] the turning back to local and state governments of the tax sources we ourselves have preempted at the federal level so that you would have those tax sources.[5]

In the meantime, the administration has announced that it will propose additional block grants in the fiscal 1983 budget. What is lacking in all of these statements is a set of guiding principles or criteria that add up to a coherent theory of federalism. The administration so far has proceeded in a piecemeal fashion and has not set forth—beyond the general statements noted above—its long-range goals concerning federalism in any detail. Specifically, which domestic program areas does the president see as basically national in scope, which as the responsibility of state or local governments, and which as candidates for shared responsibility?

Understandably, the economic situation and the difficult struggles over budget and tax cuts will almost completely monopolize the time and attention of top White House planners for much of the administration's first year in office. But beginning with the major policy statements for fiscal 1983 that must come in the president's state of the union address and budget message in January, the administration will find further piecemeal block-grant proposals difficult to defend substantively and politically unless it is prepared to lay out a coherent, comprehensive strategy for reordering the responsibilities of the federal, state, and local governments.

The Case for a Bold Move

The case for the president's boldly moving to assume leadership of a major restructuring of federal priorities and responsibilities can be made on grounds both of general public interest and of the administration's own political interests.

If, as many believe, the Reagan presidency will result in the "most radical shift in domestic policy since the New Deal," then it is in the interest of the public and in the interest of the democratic process thoroughly to air the issues in a national debate. The substantive terms of that debate can be set only by the president; they should deal not with the complicated details of budget items or the

[5] President Ronald Reagan, quoted in Lou Cannon and Helen Dewar, "Reagan Asks $48 Billion Budget Curb," *Washington Post*, March 10, 1981.

arcane judgments about different federal grant forms, but with the larger issues related to the nature, form, and division of responsibilities of the American federal system in the 1980s.

Politically, the time may be ripe for bold presidential initiatives. In 1972, a period of political stasis in national politics began as relatively weak presidents struggled in vain against the fragmentation in Congress and the power of narrowly focused special interest groups. Though it created more than 200 narrow categorical programs during the 1970s, Congress persistently showed itself incapable of reaching decisions on large issues such as welfare, health financing, energy, and economic policy.

Unlike his immediate predecessors, President Reagan has shown himself to be an extraordinarily able communicator with the public and—thus far—an adroit political operator. The outcome remains uncertain, but the president's successful seizure of the initiative in the budget and tax areas may signal the beginning of the restoration of White House power and authority. After the fiscal and economic questions are settled, an obvious next step would be to move swiftly to launch and control a debate on the federal role in the American political system.

The contrasting approaches and experiences of the Carter and Nixon administrations in addressing major governmental structural reform are relevant to the situation the Reagan administration faces. President Carter made government reorganization a major campaign issue in 1976 and gave it high priority in 1977. The Carter administration, possibly attempting to make a virtue of necessity, made much of the fact that it had no grand design for reorganization and that it would proceed through incremental, step-by-step changes. The Carter administration hoped by this means to limit the opposition of outside interest groups and of congressional committees, whose jurisdictional authority would be threatened. But ultimately, the incremental approach caused more problems than it solved. President Carter's Reorganization Task Force found that it could not proceed very far toward large-scale reorganization without encountering what might be called the "unraveling effect": Major shifts in one program area or agency not only have immediate implications for that program or agency but also often have substantial implications for other programs and agencies. For instance, if, in order to create a Department of Natural Resources, the National Oceanographic and Atmospheric Administration were removed from the Commerce Department, and, in order to create a Department of Community and Economic Development, the Economic Development Administration were also removed from the Commerce Department, where would that leave Commerce? Thus, developing a rationale for natural resource and community development consolidation would result in the need to construct a defense either of a revised department for commercial and business activities or of the nonnecessity for such an entity at the cabinet level. Because it often lacked answers to a number of the questions and issues, the Carter administration found itself vulnerable to opposing interest groups and congressional committees, which, despite the incremental approach, were implacably negative, and which, through a shrewd use of rumor and conjecture, were able to distort the administration's goals and purposes to their own advantage. In failing to develop a picture of what the federal government would look like when reorganization had been implemented, the Carter administration badly undercut its own efforts.

The Nixon administration, in marked contrast, moved steadily from 1969 to 1972 toward a comprehensive view of the federal structure. In its final form, the "new federalism" exhibited a continuum from a highly centralized federal structure—run from the White House and four supercabinet departments—down to general and special revenue sharing for the state and local governments, with federal regional councils as connecting links.

The Nixon cabinet reorganization proposals and the plans for a sweeping revision of the federal grant system with revenue sharing challenged huge numbers of interest groups and almost every committee in Congress. But the Nixon administration—until the impact of Watergate seriously weakened it on all fronts—acted from a position of strength, and the coherence and completeness of its approach contributed to that strength. And while there can be no test case or definitive conclusion, it is likely that had not Watergate intervened, President Nixon would have succeeded in achieving many of his reorganizational goals. At the end of a stasis-ridden decade, a comprehensive program to reform the system of federalism, built on a strong intellectual foundation, might well place the Reagan administration in an equally strong position to achieve its goals.

Henny Penny versus Pollyanna. There are those who think that calls for a major sorting out or reordering of responsibilities in the federal system are both unrealistic and wrongheaded. In his recent articles and lectures, Richard Nathan has espoused this view. Nathan, taking aim particularly at the analyses and recommendations which have emanated from ACIR, writes that ACIR leads the "Henny-Penny school of federalism which holds that the sky is falling, [and] thus we urgently need to adopt basic institutional and programmatic reforms."[6]

Nathan holds that proposals for a major sorting out of responsibilities stem from an oversimplistic view of government. He concludes:

> The arguments sound good and sometimes are made effectively. But we have to remember what Morton Grodzins taught us twenty-five years ago. The federal system has always been a system of *shared* responsibilities. . . . The idea of some tidy rearrangement where some functions belong to the central government, some to the states and some to local governments is attractive, but the world of government, not to mention the rest of the world, is more complicated than that. . . . I would just say that the "Henny-Penny" school tends to reach for simplistic and holistic reforms of the government system that do not fit the values underlying this system.[7]

As noted previously, if ACIR leads the "Henny-Penny" school of federal aid reform, then Nathan could be caricatured as leading the "Pollyanna" school of Alexander Pope, which comes close to arguing that "Whatever is, is right." Certainly any kind of push-button theory of the division of responsibility that assumes a neat—and complete—division is unrealistic. But it is also true that a more rational system assigning each partner in the federation predominance of authority in particular program areas and allowing shared responsibilities for special situations can be constructed. Nathan himself has argued for the federalization of welfare (see below) on the basis of certain criteria regarding the nature of income-maintenance programs and on a judgment of the strengths and weaknesses of having each federal partner—federal, state, or local—assume predominant responsibility. Judgments such as this can also be made for other important domestic program areas.

As an example of the difficulty of achieving a rational, tidy division of responsibility, Nathan has recently cited the case of federal subsidies for local transit operating costs.[8] This is, he states, clearly a local concern, and the Reagan administration is proposing to phase out this subsidy over a five-year period. The Reagan phase-

[6] Richard P. Nathan, "Reforming the Federal Grants-in-Aid System for States and Localities" (address delivered to the National Tax Association, Washington, D.C., May 18, 1981), p. 8.
[7] Ibid., pp. 8–9.
[8] Ibid., pp. 9–10.

out is misguided, however, because these operating grants have become one of the most important sources of external support for many of the older urban centers that have the most serious fiscal and social problems. Money for these urban centers, not the reason it comes nor the source from which it comes, is the key issue. Equity, he thus argues, in this case should supersede tidiness and rationality.

Yet there could hardly be a better example than this of the need for a more rational ordering of responsibilities. It is clearly impossible for the federal government to make sensible judgments based on a deep knowledge of local conditions regarding the level or scope of local transit operating subsidies. Federal takeover of more truly national concerns (such as welfare), however, would free dollars at the state and local levels, dollars which could be more efficiently used by these governments to address state and local problems, including subsidization of local transit systems if that proved wise or necessary.

A final, important point regarding the current "marbleized" federal system is that the system is based on and has been nurtured by a level of federal resources that will no longer be sustainable in the coming years. The current economic condition of the country and the Reagan administration's first budget have already begun the process of revising federal priorities and responsibilities. It is likely that again and again during the 1980s the federal government will have to make a distinction between programs which are fundamentally necessary to sustain the social and economic fabric of the country and those which are both laudable and worthwhile but are not of the same order of priority. This theme was particularly stressed by the recently published report of the President's Commission for a National Agenda for the Eighties. In the opening chapter, the report stated:

> As we enter the Eighties . . . [a] new constellation of factors—both domestic and international—has arisen . . . that requires the nation to make some fundamental choices. We no longer have the luxury of recommending more of the same in a variety of areas. . . . The nation faces a decade of difficult choices and priority-setting among many important and compelling goals . . . [and it] cannot proceed on all fronts at once.[9]

Toward a Hierarchy of Federal Responsibilities

Previous periods of reform have already placed the federal government in a commanding role in key areas of human need. The social

---

[9] President's Commission for a National Agenda for the Eighties, *A National Agenda for the Eighties* (Washington, D.C., 1980), p. 1.

security and Medicare programs provide income security and health care for the elderly; unemployment insurance guarantees a floor under the unemployed; food stamps and other nutrition programs have done much to stem hunger and malnutrition; and low-income housing programs, for all the difficulties that attend them, do represent a major federal commitment to provide decent housing for all citizens.

The administration has acknowledged and accepted this social program inheritance and has committed itself to sustaining that inheritance. Thus, the first criterion applied to the establishment of the fiscal 1982 budget priorities related to social safety nets. The budget stated:

> The first criterion is the preservation of the social safety net. The social safety net consists of those programs, mostly begun in the 1930s, that now constitute an agreed-upon core of protections for the elderly, the unemployed, the poor, and those programs that fulfill our basic commitment to the people who serve the country in times of war.[10]

There are two major national social problems, however, that remain unsolved: welfare and an adequate health-care (financing) system for all citizens. The case for a large—though not monopolistic—federal role in these two areas is quite strong, and any reshuffling of authority among the three levels of government should provide for a substantial national policy and financing responsibility.

The assumption by the federal government of a major role in welfare and health care would mean that national responsibility would have been asserted for the most basic human needs of the *general* population: food, health care, income and employment security, and housing. These would then constitute the "agreed-upon core of protections" and have first call on federal resources.

With these floors established for the support of basic human needs for the general population, the special needs of special populations occupy a second level of priority and should be dealt with largely by the state and local governments.

The establishment of a hierarchy of federal priorities has direct implications for the issues raised by both the proponents and the opponents of the Reagan administration's moves toward block grants and toward a phaseout of many existing categorical aid programs. The assertion of ever-expanding new rights, or entitlements, over the past decade and a half is rooted in the authorizing legislation for the hundreds of categorical programs created during that time.

[10] U.S., Office of Management and Budget, *Fiscal 1982 Budget Revisions* (Washington, D.C., March 1981), p. 8.

Opponents of the Reagan administration block grants and budget cuts have come close to asserting that most, if not all, of these individual grants have conferred immutable rights on their beneficiaries and that Reagan's policy would violate a moral compact between the government and the eligible populations. OMB Director Stockman, however, faces the opposite direction, asserting that he does not believe that there is "any basic right to legal services or any other kinds of service, and the idea that's been established over the last ten years that almost every service that someone might need in life ought to be provided, financed by the Government as a matter of basic right, is wrong."[11]

What is being proposed here is a middle way, a framework for establishing a clearer division of authority among all levels of government at a time of limited public resources. The federal government should expand the "agreed-upon core of protections"—federal entitlements—to encompass the basic life-support needs of the general population. Specifically, as a part of any tradeoffs between the federal government and the states and localities, the Reagan administration should take the lead in shaping welfare-reform and health-care-financing proposals in ways that provide for federal policy leadership and financing, though not necessarily for federal administrative control.

Once the federal government has moved to phase in these national social programs, there should be a hard look at its current overextended responsibilities in a number of other areas—in community and economic development, transportation, education, environmental protection, health, natural resources, law enforcement, social services, libraries, and arts and humanities.

Expansion of national foundations for the basic "agreed-upon protection" would allow the administration to argue plausibly and credibly that many worthy individual categorical programs—for example, community health centers, foster care and adoption assistance, special education programs for handicapped children, family planning, emergency medical service, black lung clinics, and fluoridation—must form a second order of priority. Such a reevaluation would not mean that all of the programs would die—there might be strong programmatic or political arguments for the retention of a Head Start program or a migrant health center—but it would mean that funding and support for them would depend on the resources available after the needs of the "agreed-upon core of protections" had been met by the federal government.

---

[11] David A. Stockman, OMB director, in *Issues and Answers* transcript (New York: ABC News, March 22, 1981), p. 18.

Criteria. This monograph is not the place for a detailed analysis and exposition of the criteria for deciding which program areas (and which individual programs) should be turned over to state and local governments. In any case, the political process will dictate a combination of factors to be taken into account. A good starting point would be a serious attempt to evaluate each program area with respect to the economists' criteria of externalities. Where spillovers are large—disease control, research, parks and recreation—more centralized financing and administration would be called for; and where they are small or medium-sized—libraries, streets, mass transit, sewage and refuse disposal—decentralized financing and administration by state or local governments would be used. Second, historical and current funding patterns by the three levels of government, as ACIR has suggested, should be taken into account: that is, program areas already heavily funded by a level of government would become prime candidates for full takeover by that government. Thus welfare and social insurance programs would be candidates for full federal responsibility. Candidates for termination of federal support would—because they are largely supported by state and local governments—include hospitals, education, and police and fire protection.

A third factor would be the strengths and weaknesses of each level of government. The federal government, for instance, remains the most efficient and equitable collector of taxes, but it remains inflexible and inefficient in the delivery of many services. Thus, income transfer programs—social security, unemployment insurance, housing assistance—under this breakdown would become candidates for full federal takeover, while the myriad of social service programs now supported by the federal government (largely through other institutions and organizations) would be left to the other two levels of government.

Finally, pragmatically, one would have to take into account the specific offers made by the National Governors Association and the National Conference of State Legislatures. The governors and state legislators have recommended a tradeoff of welfare and Medicaid costs for state and local assumptions of full financing of highways, education, and law enforcement.

The Case for a Federal Role in the Welfare and Income-Security Programs

The issues related to welfare reform have been fully debated over the past decade and will not be discussed here in any detail. It suffices to say that the rationale for a major—though not necessarily monopolistic—federal role and presence remains strong. The rationale is one of equity and efficiency and of a sensible partnership among the three levels of government.

In our highly mobile society, the spillover effects of poverty across state lines are such that a uniform minimum level of transfer payments to individuals (adjusted for cost-of-living variations) is called for, both to ensure that all citizens will be treated equally regardless of the happenstance of residence and to avoid a needless competition among the states that would distort growth and job patterns. In addition, there are substantial efficiencies in administration to be realized today through the use of computer technology to construct uniform record systems that limit fraud and waste.

In the winter 1980 issue of *Common Sense,* the magazine of the Republican National Committee, there occurred a brief, but instructive, debate regarding welfare reform among three Republicans: Richard P. Nathan, who had served as assistant director of the OMB (1969–1971) and as deputy under secretary of the Department of Health, Education, and Welfare (HEW) in 1971; Paul H. O'Neill, who had served as deputy director of the OMB (1974–1977); and Robert Carleson, who is now special assistant to the president for human resources.[12] Nathan and O'Neill argued for the necessity of a substantial federal role; Carleson made the case for a minimal federal presence, limited to the provision of virtually unrestricted block grants to the states.

Calling more for a "return to first principles" than any specifically detailed solution, O'Neill stated that:

> There are three strong, related reasons for a federal role. First, the needy population is not uniformly distributed among the states. Second, the financial capacity to aid the needy is not uniformly distributed in relation to where the needy live. Third, the federal government provides such a large share of the financial support for the existing programs that it is difficult to see how it can completely extricate itself.[13]

It becomes the role of the federal government to establish broad national policy because "the federal government is the only institution that reflects the combined judgment of our population." Specifically, O'Neill posited that the federal government should decide the total amounts of money that would be made available for the needy population and the definitions of eligibility for that money. The federal government, however, should delegate to the states

[12] Carla A. Hills (moderator), Richard P. Nathan, Robert R. Carleson, and Paul H. O'Neill, "Welfare Reform: Federalism or Federalization," *Common Sense* (Winter 1980), pp. 1–30.

[13] Ibid., p. 27.

"interpretative policy and operating responsibilities" because it is incapable of efficiently dealing with state and local variations and administrative complexities. O'Neill opposed giving the states complete freedom to develop their own programs with a system of block grants because, he stated, that would allow them to "design a program that voided the thrust of intended federal policy."[14]

Through a somewhat different path, Nathan arrived at much the same conclusions as O'Neill. He associated himself with a "sensible framework" for domestic policymaking that came out of the "new federalism" of the Nixon and Ford administrations. This framework consisted, Nathan stated, of two ideas: decentralization and the sorting-out of the functions that belong to the three levels of government. General revenue sharing and consolidated block grants were examples of decentralization policies meant to strengthen state and local governments. The sorting-out proposed by the two administrations was that service functions—education, social services, and community development, for instance—would be primarily the responsibilities of state and local governments, while income transfer programs for individuals—such as social security, Medicare, food stamps, and veterans' benefits—would be structured under uniform and equitable federal policies.

Like O'Neill, Nathan saw a role for the states in administering transfer-payment programs. "The best long-run answer," he wrote, "is to have the policies for transfer payments made at the national level, with the federal government providing equalized grant-in-aid payments to state governments which administer some of these payments."[15]

Though for somewhat different reasons than O'Neill, Nathan also opposed unrestricted block grants to states for welfare and stated:

> The idea of a block front for AFDC turns the clock back on welfare policy and would isolate the most controversial and vulnerable group of welfare recipients. It could result in competition by the states whereby some states would hold down benefits and tighten eligibility standards in ways that could eventually result in higher concentrations of the poor in the states with the most adequate welfare benefits. . . .
> The fact that people and jobs move in a free society is the underlying reason why the burden of financing welfare benefits should be shared on an equitable basis by the society as a whole.[16]

[14] Ibid., p. 29.
[15] Ibid., p. 11.
[16] Ibid., p. 10.

Robert Carleson, in holding that ultimately there is *no* federal role in the welfare area, differed fundamentally from his fellow Republicans, Nathan and O'Neill. Gliding over the problems of equity and efficiency set forth by Nathan and O'Neill, Carleson stated: "A welfare system must be designed and administered at the local level of government in order to tailor the assistance to meet the temporary needs of the community's truly needy in a timely and accurate manner."[17] The federal role would be limited initially to unrestricted block grants and eventually eliminated completely by handing over to the states some portions of federal taxing authority.

> Let the federal government make block grants to the states from the funds now spent on family assistance, food stamps, and social services and let the states design their own welfare systems. . . . The amount of the grant can be established at the level required to replace present federal funding with whatever additional amount for fiscal relief may be found necessary. That grant level, once established for a state and indexed for inflation, population changes, and unusually high unemployment, would remain in place without regard to increases or decreases in the state's caseload. . . . Eventually the federal block grants could be supplanted by state funding if the federal government would return some of its taxing authority to the states.[18]

Any move toward "uniform national standards," or "simplification of eligibility requirements," would end up not with a reformed welfare system, according to Carleson, but with a permanent system for the redistribution of income. Carleson was deeply pessimistic about the ensuing results, once such a system is in place. He stated:

> The political dynamics of a representative democracy would act to accelerate the redistribution process. Irresistible pressures would build on Congress to increase the centrally-set benefit levels. Millions of additional persons would receive . . . benefits. More pressure would then build from a greater number of constituents for benefits, another benefits increase would come and on and on, until most Americans would be receiving . . . benefits. Eventually, the nation's economic system would collapse.[19]

Carleson's pessimistic view of the ability of representative democracies to hold down and control social spending has an ironic twist in light of recent events. For instance, AFDC payments to individuals

[17] Ibid., p. 13.
[18] Ibid., pp. 17–19.
[19] Ibid., p. 15.

and families declined substantially in real dollar terms during the 1970s, because they are not indexed to inflation and have been held almost constant by federal and state governments. Data compiled by the Department of Health and Human Services show that, in constant dollars, the average monthly AFDC benefit paid to families declined by 56 percent between 1969 and 1980. Further, the Reagan administration developed powerful and bipartisan support for its budget cuts, most of which fall heavily in the domestic social areas that Carleson sees as the source of the "irresistible pressures." The very success of the president's efforts worked to undercut Carleson's 1980 prophecy. Events at the federal level in many ways followed the kind of grassroots revolt against high taxes and big spending evident at the state and local levels for several years. While the situation could change, it seems likely that at all levels of government the forces to hold down spending will remain strong for much of the decade.

Further, moving to block grants and tranferring taxing authority to the states will not accomplish the goal Carleson had in mind: removal of the federal government from major responsibility in the welfare area. With both block grants and tax transfer, Congress would still have to decide the overall level of welfare spending for the nation. Carleson stated that the block-grant level would be the "present federal funding plus whatever fiscal relief may be found necessary";[20] but he nowhere indicated on what basis Congress would decide the amount of fiscal relief. In addition, designing a tax transfer to the individual states that took into account all of the necessary economic, social, and political variables would constitute an extraordinarily difficult, if not impossible, task and would in the end be a cumbersome and inefficient method of handling this problem.

The Federal Role in Health-Care Financing

Many of the equity and efficiency arguments that are made for the federal role in welfare apply in the health-care financing area. Ironically, though the subject has often been the subject of emotional and partisan debate, the Reagan administration seems to find accepting a substantial federal role less distasteful in health than in welfare.

One of the options the administration is considering is a national health-care voucher system that would stress competition and consumer choice. Under the system—which is a variation of a plan suggested jointly by David A. Stockman, when he was a congress-

[20] Ibid., p. 19.

man, and Representative Richard Gephardt (Democrat, Missouri)—
an individual or a family would be given a voucher to apply to
competing health-care and insurance plans. The consumer would be
free to shop among various health and insurance plans; thus the
emphasis of the proposal is on competition and consumer choice.
There would, however, be an important federal role not unlike that
suggested by Paul O'Neill in the welfare area. The federal government would establish national policy by prescribing the number and
kinds of services that would constitute a minimum health plan and
set the eligibility requirements for voucher subsidies for the poor.

In a recent article, in which he described the voucher bill he has
introduced this year, Representative Gephardt stated the reasons he
was optimistic that the legislation would soon move.

> The political timing is right for such a move. Health and
> Human Services Secretary Richard S. Schweiker, who spon-
> sored a similar bill in the Senate, reports that this is a priority
> item for the Reagan Administration. That is not surprising
> since OMB Director David A. Stockman joined me last year
> in cosponsoring this legislation. . . .
>
> Certainly such a plan will get a sympathetic hearing from
> House Budget Committee Chairman James J. Jones and Sen-
> ate Health Subcommittee Chairman David Durenberger, both
> of whom have sponsored similar bills themselves. A move
> in this direction is consistent with the continuing presiden-
> tial and congressional interest in reducing regulation.
>
> It is ironic, since health care was hardly a major issue in
> the presidential campaign, to realize that Ronald Reagan's
> selection may have its most radical impact on the health
> care industry.
>
> But it is very possible that the President's interest, a con-
> tinuing concern about costs and a lot of other workable or
> attractive ideas may bring this about.[21]

Tentative Sorting-Out Proposals

Detailed analysis on particular tradeoff or sorting-out proposals is
just beginning; but several tentative proposals, along with rough
estimates of costs, have recently emerged. Two are presented here
as illustrative of potential regroupings of federal and state responsibilities. The first is a proposal developed by the ACIR, and the
second represents a joint recommendation of the National Governors

---

[21] Richard A. Gephardt, "Consumer Choice Medical Care—Needed Now," *Journal of
the Institute for Socioeconomic Studies* (Summer 1981), pp. 9–10.

Association (NGA) and the National Conference of State Legislatures (NCSL).[22] Both hinge upon a federal takeover of most or all programs in the welfare and income-security areas, but both are constructed so that they are essentially neutral in relation to the dollar amounts being traded back and forth. They also take into consideration special reasons why individual programs—for instance, bilingual education and certain programs for the handicapped—might remain federal responsibility.

The ACIR Staff Proposal. One of two alternatives developed for ACIR involves 140 existing federal aid programs and totals about $14 billion on each side of the federal-state ledger (see appendix C, table C1). The organizing principle behind the tradeoff would be to federalize all income-security cash-payment and voucher programs, while terminating most federal programs for education and medical, food, and social services.

The goal of federalization and consolidation would be to integrate in a single system four existing types of income-security programs: insurance (social security and unemployment), cash payments (welfare and supplemental-security income), in-kind benefits (housing, Medicaid, food stamps, child care, and job training), and referrals (contacts with social services and job placement).

The program integration would result in a single federal focal point for income-security programs. The consolidated programs would be administered by a network of federal offices built around the present social security office. The ACIR staff foresee a number of administrative savings through such changes as instituting a single eligibility determination for each individual or family, reducing middle-man operations with state and local governments, and consolidating numerous administrative regulations that currently emanate from at least five separate federal departments and agencies. The voucher-related programs would continue to rely on state, local, and private social service medical and housing entities for service delivery on a cost reimbursement basis.

Most of the state and local government costs being taken over by the federal government stem from cash welfare payments and Medicaid. These payments add up to about $14 billion, approximately equal to the dollars state and local governments would lose in aid to education, medical assistance, food programs (other than food stamps), and social services. (The staff proposal foresees that 20 percent of the federal social services money would remain federalized

---

[22] ACIR Staff, "Further Report on Illustrative Functional Trade-Offs," in *Docket Book*, 73rd Meeting (Washington, D.C., April 22–23, 1981), pp. 6–8.

in a child-care voucher program.) State and local governments would also retain responsibility under this plan for general assistance needs that the few consolidated federal programs would not reach (for example, local emergency relief and relief for street people). These general assistance programs would amount to about $1.2 billion.

The proposal also takes into account that there are special reasons why some programs should be retained at the federal level. These programs include research—medical and educational research and research for which there is a special federal obligation—and aid to the handicapped, Indians, migrant farm workers, and aliens. In the area of education, the Head Start program and certain bilingual programs would remain federal responsibilities. (See appendix C, table C3 for a list of programs to be federalized, those to go to the states, and those to be retained by the federal government.)

The NGA Proposal. The NGA for several years has been calling for a large-scale sorting out of federal, state, and local responsibilities. In November 1980, just after the presidential election, the NGA and the NCSL issued a joint statement of support for a reorganization of roles among the levels of government and suggested specifically that the division recognize the "primary federal policy function and financial responsibility for national defense, income security and a sound economy, and the primacy of state and local governments in such areas as education, law enforcement and transportation."[23]

In a February 17, 1981, letter to all governors, Governor Bruce Babbitt (Democrat, Arizona) urged an expeditious follow-through with the Reagan administration and presented a specific proposal for a redivision of program responsibilities. He argued:

> President Reagan has told us that he places a high priority on restructuring the American union into a federation of sovereign states. . . . This unequivocal call to reform the federal system, repeated at the Detroit convention, during the campaign and again in the President's inaugural, is unparalleled in recent times. It presents to the Governors a chance to take the lead in a thorough-going reform of the federal system. . . . In recent years, [the] dual federalism system has all but disappeared. Categorical grant programs that began as modest efforts to provide supplemental assistance to local governments have evolved into instruments of federal program domination. . . . Federal invasion of state and local responsibilities will not be reversed by across-the-

---

[23] Ibid., p. 37.

board budget cuts or other forms of general fiscal reform, however desirable such reforms may be for other objectives. Dual sovereignty can be restored only by a deliberate decision to uproot and terminate federal programs in selected program areas where the states can and will carry out their historic responsibilities.[24]

Babbitt went on to lay out a specific set of tradeoffs in which the states would assume full program and fiscal responsibility for three areas: highways and mass transit, law enforcement, and elementary and secondary education. "Roads, police and schools," he stated, "are the most basic and local of governmental functions; each of these governmental functions commands broad community support and a high percentage of state and local assistance."[25]

Regarding transportation (which uses about $13 billion in federal funds), Babbitt argued that the interstate system was now about 98 percent complete and the states should assume responsibility for its upkeep as well as for the upkeep and maintenance of all other roads and bridges. The same would be true for local mass-transit programs. He stated: "It is difficult to see any overriding national interest in subsidizing local mass transit."[26] For this reason, states and localities should take over, wherever appropriate, the burden of supporting these subsidies.

In the law enforcement area ($500 million in federal aid), Babbitt argued that the Safe Streets Act of 1968 and the Law Enforcement Assistance Administration created by the act were widely acknowledged to have failed in their joint mission to lower local crime rates. "Local law enforcement," he stated, "does not lack for local support, and no one has suggested that the federal government has any particular wisdom or expertise to have an impact with its money in this area."[27]

Regarding primary and secondary education ($6 billion in federal funds), Babbitt noted that "although [federal support] is less than 10 percent of the total intergovernmental expenditures for elementary and secondary education, it has brought with it pervasive federal interference in nearly every aspect of local education." Yet, he stated, federal involvement has been accompanied by a steady decline in national scholastic achievement scores and targeted federal aid has had no measurable impact on stemming that decline. States have

[24] Ibid., pp. 35–37.
[25] Ibid., p. 35.
[26] Ibid., p. 36.
[27] Ibid., p. 36.

also moved in recent years to correct the inequities and disparities in local financing; thus, he concluded finally: "It is now time to reassert the primacy of state and local financing and control of education."[28]

On the other side of the ledger, Governor Babbitt presented the case for federal assumption of the welfare system. At Governor Babbitt's request, the ACIR staff put together a tentative ledger, backed by a list of programs to be transferred between the federal and state levels of government. (See appendix C, table C2)

Clearly there are a number of potential combinations of programs that could be included in any reshuffling of responsibilities. In addition to the budget categories stressed in the two proposals presented, other areas which have been mentioned as candidates for devolution include food and nutrition, environmental protection (the heavy federal subsidy of waste-water treatment plants), health, and community and economic development, plus a group of smaller areas that now receive federal support such as fire protection, vocational rehabilitation, libraries, and arts and humanities.

In each case, the re-sorting could be flexible and could take into account special situations warranting continued federal involvement or shared responsibilities among the federal, state, and local governments.

Recommendations

The president's 1982 state of the union message is the obvious vehicle for beginning a national dialogue and laying down a national strategy for the future of American federalism in the 1980s. In the welfare-reform and national health-insurance areas, two specific proposals are recommended here as the touchstones for public discussion: the minimum-security-income proposal advanced by the President's Commission for a National Agenda for the Eighties and the health voucher bill put forward by Representative Richard Gephardt.

The Agenda for the Eighties Commission recommended that the present assortment of income-maintenance programs—food stamps, AFDC, and housing and energy subsidies—be scrapped and in its place the federal government establish a minimum-security-income program that would provide an income of two-thirds to three-quarters of the poverty line (adjusted for regional cost-of-living differences) with a sliding tax on earnings above the poverty line. The

[28] Ibid., pp. 36–37.

chief model for this recommendation was the Family Assistance Plan first suggested by the Nixon administration. Though there are undoubtedly difficulties in adjusting the tax to produce incentives to work, the minimum-income-security plan contains elements that should attract both conservatives and liberals. For conservatives the plan would mean wiping out the large and unwieldy welfare bureaucracy, eliminating overlapping and outdated programs, and cutting administrative costs. Setting the floor somewhat below the poverty line would also allow individual states to make their own determinations about the ultimate level of support to be underwritten by public resources, given other demands on the state and local budgets. For liberals, the plan would establish income maintenance as a federally funded entitlement and shift the battle to questions relating to the adequacy of that support level.

The Gephardt (and Stockman) health-voucher system, which was also endorsed by the Agenda for the Eighties Commission, likewise encompasses elements that should prove compelling for both conservatives and liberals. For conservatives, the dependence on competitive market forces and consumer choice would form a marked contrast to the more intrusive, regulatory approach to health insurance advocated by Senator Edward M. Kennedy and a number of liberal groups and organizations. For the liberals, once again the attraction would be the establishment of a comprehensive federal role and responsibility in the area of health-care financing.

The Agenda for the Eighties Commission estimated that its minimum-security-income plan would cost the federal treasury between $15 billion and $20 billion annually. The Congressional Budget Office has estimated that the Gephardt (and Stockman) bill, over the long run, would cost about $13 billion annually. The immediate additions of these sums to the federal budget would be quite difficult, given the already overwhelming demands on the budget and the overall economic condition of the country. But to paraphrase the 1975 argument of OMB Director Stockman, there is no reason the president could not or should not announce in January 1982, his intention to "carve out a path" in the federal budget, beginning sometime in the next year or two, that would widen gradually to the approximately $35 billion needed to fund these two reforms.

At the same time, in order to make the sorting out of responsibilities a genuine two-way street—and to make way for the new programs—the president should create a mechanism for a formal discussion among the three levels of government about those program areas which would be taken over by state and local governments. The ACIR and representatives of state and local organizations

have suggested that the president convene an assembly of representatives of the federal, state, and local governments, as well as representatives of the public at large, to analyze the current state of
American federalism and then to make recommendations regarding
a redivision of responsibilities and resources. Plans for such a con-
vocation could also be an element in a proposed new strategy for
federalism announced in the state of the union message.

Conclusion

This monograph has attempted to present both the political and the
substantive cases for the president's moving out boldly in the near
future with a set of proposals that would result in a genuine sorting
out of responsibilities: a new intergovernmental partnership in which
the federal government would assume primary authority for income
maintenance and for health-care financing and the state and local
governments would assume authority and financial responsibility for
yet-to-be-determined program areas such as education, transportation, law enforcement, health and hospitals, environmental protection (particularly capital construction projects), natural resources
development, and community and economic development.

The hierarchy of priorities recommended here is not likely to
give entire satisfaction either to the administration or to the cham-
pions of new "entitlements." The administration seems to have a
visceral, ideological negative reaction to the federalization of welfare.
And many of its opponents substitute moral outrage for a rational
assessment of social priorities. But as the Agenda for the Eighties
Commission stated:

> We must face honestly the trade-offs that are inevitable
> when limited resources confront unlimited claims. . . . We
> cannot do all that we would like to reduce taxes, to increase
> living standards, to expand social programs, to improve
> national defense, to increase private investment, to solve
> environmental problems, to expand research and develop-
> ment activities, to resolve long-term energy problems and
> to reduce inflation. . . . The nation faces a decade of difficult
> choices and priority-setting among many important and
> compelling goals.[29]

[29] President's Commission for a National Agenda for the Eighties, *A National Agenda
for the Eighties*, p. 5.

Appendix A

Stockman on Reordering
National Social Priorities

In an article in *Public Interest* in 1975,[1] David A. Stockman, now director of the Office of Management and Budget, made a strong case for reordering national social-program-spending priorities and replacing the existing "social pork barrel" bound up in hundreds of categorical-grant programs with genuine social reforms: universal income maintenance and national health insurance. Stockman placed the blame for the continuance of the inefficient and inequitable system on both liberals and conservatives in Congress ("convervative duplicity and liberal ideology"). He stated: "In the main. . .the essential impediment to reprogramming the social welfare budget is deeply political and structural. The care and maintenance of the social welfare spending pipeline extend to each of the 435 Congressional districts in the nation and have now become a central preoccupation of members and their staffs. The task ranges from vigilance in committee and on the floor to ensure that allocation formulas provide maximum benefits to the district, to intervention before the agencies on behalf of local clientele groups or project applications, to ceaseless on-site inspections and the development of close working relationships with all manner of federal grantees at the local level."

Occupied with the maintenance of the myriad of narrow-purposed grants—"a grab-bag of uncoordinated, gap-ridden programs"—Congress had consistently refused to begin planning and reprogramming money for national health insurance and universal income maintenance. Stated Stockman: "While national health insurance and welfare reform have been time and again artfully deferred, Congress has not been loathe to add a billion here for black

---

[1] David A. Stockman, "The Social Pork Barrel," *Public Interest*, no. 39 (Spring 1975), pp. 3–30.

lung compensation. . .or a billion extra there for disaster relief. . . .
It has persistently refused to phase out federal funding for community mental health center programs [and] it raises each year's
appropriation for the National Cancer Institute."

The time had come, Stockman argued, to break through the
"political sinews" of the iron triangle of special interest groups,
agency bureaucrats, and congressional protectors and to institute a
"fundamental shift in social policy strategy." That shift would reor-
der national social spending priorities by legislating a universal income-maintenance program and national health insurance. Stockman
further argued that it was "illusory" to think that funds for these
new social advances could be obtained by reordering other current
spending priorities (shifting money from defense, highways, space
programs, or farm subsidies) or by tax reform. The money would
have to come from reprogramming within the social budget itself—
by jettisoning many of the existing social-service-oriented categorical
grant programs. He stated that

> the explicitly service-oriented programs—compensatory ed-
> ucation, community mental health centers, vocational re-
> habilitation, social services—that fall under the social spending
> umbrella have yet to demonstrate any clear effectiveness
> and are most notable for their almost random distribution
> of benefits among a tiny fraction of the formally entitled
> population.
> Given current fiscal realities, there is equally little doubt
> how any fundamental policy redirections must be financed.
> A decisive shift toward alternative strategies—a compre-
> hensive national health-insurance program and universal
> income maintenance—can be accomplished only through a
> vast reprogramming of funds from *within* the social welfare
> sector of the budget itself. . . . At least in terms of sheer
> arithmetic, there is no reason in the world why a budget
> path, widening to something like the $30 billion to $50 billion
> in incremental financing that would be needed for these
> new programs when fully effective, could not be carved out
> of the 1978 social welfare budget, were an effort now begun
> to pave the way.

Appendix B

Programs Included in Block Grants

TABLE B1

PROGRAMS INCLUDED IN BLOCK GRANTS
(millions of dollars)

Program	1981 Current Services	1982 Budget Request
Health Services Block Grant		
Community Health Centers:		
Primary Health Care Centers	325	
Primary Health Care	7	
Black Lung Services	5	
Migrant Health	44	
Home Health Services	4	
Maternal and Child Health:		
Grants to States	357	
SSI	30	
Hemophilia	3	
Sudden Infant Death Syndrome	3	
Emergency Medical Services	30	
Program Management	34	
Mental Health and Substance Abuse Services:		
Mental Health Services	324	
Drug Abuse Project Grants & Contracts	161	
Drug Abuse Grants to States	30	
Alcoholism Project Grants & Contracts	73	
Alcoholism Grants to States	50	
Program Management	57	
Total Health Services Block Grant	1,537	1,138

TABLE B1—Continued

Program	1981 Current Services	1982 Budget Request
Preventive Health Services Block Grant:		
High Blood Pressure Control	20	
Health Incentive Grants	36	
Risk Reduction & Health Education	16	
Venereal Disease	40	
Immunization	24	
Fluoridation	5	
Rat Control	13	
Lead-Based Paint Poisoning Prevention	10	
Genetic Diseases	13	
Family Planning Services	166	
Adolescent Health Services	10	
Total Preventive Health Services Block Grant	353	260
Federal Administrative Costs		1
Total Public Health Service Block Grants	1,890	1,400
Social Services Block Grant		
Title XX Social Services	2,716	
Title XX Day Care	200	
Title XX State & Local Training	75	
Child Welfare Services	163	
Child Welfare Training	6	
Foster Care	349	
Adoption Assistance	10	
Child Abuse	7	
Runaway Youth	10	
Developmental Disabilities	51	
OHDS Salaries and Expenses	4	
Rehabilitation Services	931	
Community Services Administration	483	
Total Social Services Block Grant	5,005	3,800
Emergency Assistance Block Grant		
Emergency Assistance	55	
Hardship Energy Assistance	1,850	
Total Emergency Assistance Block Grant	1,905	1,399
Grand Total Block Grants	8,800	6,600
(Outlays)		(5,400)

SOURCE: Office of Management and Budget.

TABLE B2

ANTECEDENT PROGRAMS OF THE ELEMENTARY AND SECONDARY
EDUCATION CONSOLIDATION ACT
(millions of dollars)

	1981 Continuing Resolution	1981 Revised Request	1982 Revised Request
Local Education Block Grant: Title I: Financial Assistance to Meet Special Educational Needs			
Grants for Disadvantaged (Elementary and Secondary Education Act, Title I)			
Basic Grants to Local Educational Agencies (Section 111)	2,824.9	2,118.7	
Concentration Grants (Section 117)	142.1	106.6	
State Agency Migrant Grants (Sections 143, 144)	288.0	216.0	
State Agency Handicapped Grants (Section 146)	165.0	123.8	
State Agency Neglected and Delinquent Grants (Section 151, 153)	37.8	28.3	
Emergency School Aid (Emergency School Aid Act)			
Basic Grants to Local Educational Agencies (Section 606a)	107.8	80.9	
Special Programs and Projects (Section 608a)	75.1	56.3	
Magnet Schools, Pairing and Neutral Site Schools (Section 608 [a] [1], [2], [3])	30.0	22.5	
Education for Handicapped (Education for the Handicapped Act)			
State Grant Program (Part B, Section 611)	922.0	691.5	
Preschool Incentive Grants (Part B, Section 619)	25.0	18.7	
Adult Education (Adult Education Act)			
Grants to States (Section 304)	120.0	90.0	
Subtotal, Title I (ESECA)	4,737.7	3,553.3	3,790.1

TABLE B2—Continued

	1981 Continuing Resolution	1981 Revised Request	1982 Revised Request
State Education Block Grant:			
Title II: Financial Assistance for Improvement of School Resources and Performance			
Grants for Disadvantaged (Elementary and Secondary Education Act, Title I)			
State Administration (Section 194)	47.0	35.3	
Evaluation (Section 183)	8.0	5.4	
Improving Local Educational Practice (Elementary and Secondary Education Act, Title IV-C)	91.4	50.0	
Strengthening State Educational Management (Elementary and Secondary Education Act, Title V-B)	51.0	38.3	
Emergency School Aid (Emergency School Aid Act)			
Special Programs and Projects (Section 608a)	8.5	6.4	
Grants to Nonprofit Organizations (Section 608b)	7.5	5.6	
Educational Television and Radio (Section 611)	6.4	4.8	
Training and Advisory Services (Civil Rights Act, Title IV)	45.7	34.3	
Women's Educational Equity (Elementary and Secondary Education Act, Title IX-C)	10.0	7.5	
School Libraries and Instructional Resources (Elementary and Secondary Education Act, Title IV-B)	171.0	128.2	
Education for the Handicapped (Education for the Handicapped Act)			
Severely Handicapped (Part C, Sections 621 and 624)	5.0	3.8	
Early Childhood Education (Part C, Section 623)	18.8	13.8	
Regional Vocational, Adult, and Postsecondary Programs (Part C, Section 625)	2.2	1.2	

TABLE B2—Continued

	1981 Continuing Resolution	1981 Revised Request	1982 Revised Request
Innovation and Development	7.8	2.8	
Regional Resource Centers (Part C, Section 621)	9.8	7.3	
Special Education Personnel Development (Part D, Section 631, 632, 634)	58.0	43.5	
Career Education Incentives (P.L. 95–207, Section 4)	14.8	9.9	
Community Schools (Elementary and Secondary Education Act, Title VIII, Sections 809, 810, 812)	10.0	3.1	
Consumers' Education (Elementary and Secondary Education Act, Title III-E)	3.6	2.7	
Law-related Education (Elementary and Secondary Education Act, Title III-G)	1.0	0.7	
Basic Skills Improvement (Elementary and Secondary Education Act, Title II)			
State Grants Programs	13.4	11.4	
Discretionary Programs	18.1	12.6	
Follow Through (Headstart–Follow Through Act)	35.2	28.2	
Gifted and Talented (Elementary and Secondary Education Act, Title IX-A)	5.4	3.8	
Alcohol and Drug Abuse Education (Alcohol and Drug Abuse Education Act)	3.0	2.2	
Arts in Education (Elementary and Secondary Education Act, Title III-C)	3.5	2.6	
Metric Education (Elementary and Secondary Education Act, Title III-B)	1.7	1.3	
Ethnic Heritage Studies (Elementary and Secondary Education Act, Title IX-E)	3.0	2.2	
Cities in Schools (Elementary and Secondary Education Act, Title III-A, Section 303 [d] [1])	3.0	2.3	

TABLE B2—Continued

	1981 Continuing Resolution	1981 Revised Request	1982 Revised Request
PUSH for Excellence (Elementary and Secondary Education Act, Title III-A, Section 303 [d] [1])	1.0	.7	
Teacher Corps (Higher Education Act, Title V-A)	29.0	21.5	
Teacher Centers (Higher Education Act, Section 532)	13.0	9.8	
Pre-College Science Teacher Training (National Science Foundation Act of 1950)	2.5	1.9	
Subtotal, Title II (ESECA)	709.3	505.1	565.1
Total, Elementary and Secondary Education Consolidation Act	5,447.0	4,058.4	4,355.2

SOURCE: Office of Management and Budget.

Appendix C

Proposals for Federal Programs to Be Traded,
Transferred, Terminated, or Retained and
Consolidated

TABLE C1
A Limited Federal Aid Trade-Off Example
(dollars)

	Federalized Income Security Programs (Federal Funding Pick-up)	Terminated Programs (Federal Funding Loss)	
Cash Payments to Individuals			
Insurance			
Social Security	0	Education	4,032,954
Unemployment	226,000		
Cash Payments			
Public Assistance (HHS)[a]	7,000,000		
Work Incentives (HHS)	37,202		
SSI[b] (HHS)	1,670,991		
Vouchers or Direct Payments to Vendors			
Housing Vouchers	0		
Weatherization (Energy)[a]	0		
Emergency Energy (CSA)[a]	8,000	Other Medical Assistance	2,452,625
Medicaid (HHS)	4,542,048	Food (other than Food Stamps)	4,543,398
Food Stamps (Ag)[a]	362,570		
Job Training			
CETA (Labor)[a]	0	Social Services, etc. (except Child Care)	2,793,630
Vocational Rehabilitation (HHS)	0		
Child Care (HHS)	123,750		

Incidental Services	0	
Integrated Eligibility Determination		
Counseling	0	
Job Placement (Labor)	0	
Total	13,970,561	13,822,607

[a] Initials or words in parentheses stand for:
Ag: Department of Agriculture
CSA: Community Services Administration
Energy: Department of Energy
HHS: Department of Health and Human Services
Labor: Department of Labor.
[b] SSI: Supplemental Security Income.
SOURCE: Advisory Commission on Intergovernmental Regulations.

TABLE C2

POTENTIAL TRADE-OFF: FEDERALIZING WELFARE IN EXCHANGE FOR
TERMINATING MOST FEDERAL AID IN LAW ENFORCEMENT,
EDUCATION, AND HIGHWAYS
(thousands of dollars)

Program	FY 1980 Total	Total to Be Terminated
FEDERAL AID FUNDING TO BE TERMINATED		
Law Enforcement (grants to state and local governments)		
Juvenile Justice	100,000	100,000
Education		
Elementary and Secondary	5,897,005	
Higher	304,829	
Vocational	704,227	
Research	378,421	
Other	61,135	
Total	7,345,617	4,032,957[a]
Highways		
Interstate	3,900,000	
Primary	1,800,000	
Rural	600,000	
Urban	800,000	
Bridges	1,700,000	
Miscellaneous	400,000	9,200,000
Total	9,200,000	13,332,957
PROGRAMS TO BE ASSUMED BY FEDERAL GOVERNMENT		
Welfare (broadly defined)		
AFDC	7,000,000	
SSI	1,670,991	
Food Stamps	362,570	
Unemployment	226,000	
Work Incentives	37,202	
Emergency Energy Assistance	8,000	
Medicaid	4,542,048	
Child Care	123,750	
Total	13,970,561[b]	13,970,561

[a] Specific programs to be terminated and retained are listed in table C4.
[b] A broader scope of income security programs, including housing, medical, and employment aids. See table C3.
SOURCE: Advisory Commission on Intergovernmental Regulations.

TABLE C3

Programs to Be Federalized
(dollars)

Federal Aid Cluster	FY 1980 Funding
1. Housing	
Lower Income Housing Assistance	20,045,328
Farm Labor Housing	55,000
2. Medical Assistance	
Medical Aid	12,616,799
Migrant Health	41,400
4. Employment and Training	
Comprehensive Planning and Training	8,201,207
Unemployment Insurance	2,034,600
State Employment Services	753,100
Work Incentives	372,023
Employment of Seasonal Farmworkers	87,295
Native American Employment and Training	78,566
5. Public Assistance	
Public Assistance (AFDC and Aid to Disabled)	7,056,710
Social Services (Title XX)	2,475,000[a]
Weatherization Assistance for Low-Income Persons	198,750
Emergency Energy Conservation	40,000
Public Assistance Payments Research	3,500
7. Food and Nutrition	
Food Stamps	6,401,000
State Administration of Food Stamps	362,570
13. Vocational Rehabilitation	
Rehabilitation Services and Facilities	417,484
Vocational Rehabilitation for Disabled	113,680
Handicapped Personnel Preparation	55,375
Vocational Rehabilitation for SSI Recipients	55,000
Rehabilitation Training	30,500
Handicapped Media	19,000
Deaf/Blind Centers for Children	16,000
Rehabilitation Services, Expansion	11,775

[a] × 80 percent (Child Care).
Source: Advisory Commission on Intergovernmental Regulations.

TABLE C4

Programs to Be Terminated
(dollars)

Federal Aid Cluster	FY 1980 Funding
2. MEDICAL ASSISTANCE	
Community Health Centers	319,483
Maternal and Child Health Services	255,300
Community Mental Health Centers	194,673
Health Maintenance Organizations	152,540
Drug Abuse Community Service	147,385
Family Planning	138,885
Crippled Children Services	102,100
Mental Health Clinical and Service Training	70,663
State Health Care Survey Certification	69,645
Disease Control	65,532
Alcoholism Treatment and Rehabilitation	64,572
Alcohol Abuse	56,800
State Medical Fraud Control	55,899
Public Health Service	52,000
Drug Abuse	40,000
Medical Facilities Construction	39,855
Emergency Medical Services	36,625
Family Medicine Graduate Training	30,500
Appalachian Health	23,700
Veterans State Nursing Home Care	22,529
Health Careers Opportunity	19,000
Mental Health, Children's Services	14,830
Nurse Practitioner Training	13,000
Hypertension Treatment	13,000
Community Care for Alcoholism, Uniform Act	12,127
Physician Assistant Training	9,100
Nursing Scholarships	9,000
Drug Abuse, Clinical and Service Related	7,978
State Nursing Home Care for Veterans, Construction	5,867
Health Professions, Financial Distress of Schools	5,000
Drug Abuse	4,960
Veterans State Hospital	4,871
Drug Abuse Education	4,705
Alcohol Clinical Service and Training	4,075
Genetic Disease Testing and Counseling	4,000
Alcohol Abuse Prevention Demonstration	3,059
Emergency Medical Services Training	3,000
Hemophilia Diagnostic Treatment Centers	3,000

Federal Aid Cluster	FY 1980 Funding
Alcohol and Drug Abuse Education	3,000
Sudden Infant Death Information and Counseling	2,802
Medical Health Hospital Improvement	1,900
Home Health Services and Training	804
Mental Health Hospital Staff Development	325
4. EMPLOYMENT AND TRAINING	
Youth Employment and Training	797,974
Summer Youth Employment	533,225
Job Corps	415,700
Employment for the Disadvantaged	162,740
Youth Employment, Community Conservation	134,008
Youth Employment, Entitlement Pilot	107,100
Youth Conservation Corps	24,790
Youth Conservation Service Corps	18,000
Older Persons Opportunities	10,500
5. PUBLIC ASSISTANCE	
Social Services (Title XX except Child Care)	2,474,000[a]
Child Support Enforcement	333,000
Aging Assistance	219,470
Public Assistance Training (Title XX)	100,825
Child Welfare Services	56,500
Public Assistance Training	31,000
Aging Services	30,000
Aging, Training Workers	17,000
Runaway Youth Facilities	11,000
Senior Companion Program	8,135
Child Welfare Services and Training	5,000
Anti-Poverty Mini-Grants for Volunteer Programs	1,700
7. FOOD AND NUTRITION	
School Lunch	2,123,100
Surplus Food Distribution—sale, exchange	813,535
Special Supplemental Food for Women and Children	750,000
Nutrition for the Aging	254,546
School Breakfasts, Grants to States	224,800
Child Care, Food	213,000
Summer Food for Children	135,800
Child Nutrition, State Expenses	34,867
Milk for Children	32,000
Equipment for School Food Services	20,000
Nutrition, Education and Training	20,000

TABLE C4—Continued

Federal Aid Cluster	FY 1980 Funding
Nutrition Education	1,750
Community Food and Nutrition	28,000
10. EDUCATION	
Elementary and Secondary	
Grants for Educationally Deprived Children	2,625,594
Federal Impact School Aid	483,000
Local Education Improvement	197,400
Education of Children in State Institutions	37,500
Right to Read	35,000
Guidance Counseling and Testing in Elementary and Secondary Schools	18,000
Appalachian Child Development	10,000
Humanities Promotion in Elementary and Secondary Education	4,500
Education of Gifted Youth	3,780
Art Education in Elementary and Secondary Schools	1,250
Higher Education	
Adult Education	100,000
Higher Education Land Grants	11,500
Higher Education Equipment	7,500
Humanities Promotion in Higher Education	5,000
Humanities Promotion in Higher Education	4,400
Humanities Promotion in Higher Education, Pilot Grant	2,000
Higher Education Academic Facilities	500
Vocational	
Vocational Education, Basic Grants to States	475,096
Vocational Education	113,317
Consumer and Homemaking Education	43,432
Other	
Teacher Corps	37,500
Teacher Centers Inservice Training	13,000
Environmental Education	3,500
Consumer Education	3,135
Citizen Education, Cultural	3,000
Telecommunications for Delivering Health, Education, and Social Services	1,000

ª × 80 percent.
SOURCE: Advisory Commission on Intergovernmental Regulations.

TABLE C5

PROGRAMS TO BE RETAINED/CONSOLIDATED
(dollars)

Federal Aid Cluster	FY 1980 Funding
1. HOUSING	
Public Housing	2,082,500
Public Housing, modernization	409,200
Appalachian Housing	9,600
Rural Self Help Housing	5,000
2. MEDICAL ASSISTANCE	
Health Resource Planning	107,000
Coal Miners Respiratory Impairment Clinics	75,000
Health Financing Research	51,282
State Health Planning	30,000
Health Services Research and Development	25,907
Family Planning Training	3,000
Alcoholism Demonstration and Evaluation	1,490
Drug Abuse Research Scientist Development	1,370
Nursing Education Research	1,101
Maternal and Child Health Research	1,000
Alcohol Research Scientist Development	986
4. EMPLOYMENT AND TRAINING	
Community Service Employment, Older Americans	234,800
EEOC Enforcement	18,500
Employment and Training Research	14,300
5. PUBLIC ASSISTANCE	
Native American Self Sufficiency	33,800
Child Abuse and Neglect, Prevention, Treatment	18,928
Child Welfare Administration and Research	13,230
Veterans State Domiciliary Care	12,301
Aging Research	8,500
Social Services Research and Demonstration	5,975
Adoption Practices Improvement	5,000
Public Assistance Payments Research	3,500
Youth Development Research (that is, runaway youth)	1,470
10. EDUCATION	
Elementary and Secondary	
Education of Handicapped Children	804,000
Head Start	700,000
Education of Migrant Children	209,000
Emergency School Aid for Minority Children	150,000

TABLE C5—Continued

Federal Aid Cluster	FY 1980 Funding
Education for Handicapped Children	143,000
Emergency School Aid for Minorities	137,600
Elementary and Secondary School Minority Aid	95,769
Civil Rights Technical Assistance for Schools	52,700
Disadvantaged Children Education Aid	50,794
Development Disabilities Services	49,880
Indian Education	47,273
Indian Education	15,000
Educational TV for Minorities	9,858
Developmental Disabilities	5,557
Education for Severely Handicapped	5,000
Regional Education for Deaf or Other Handicapped	2,400
Handicapped Teacher Recruitment and Information	1,000
Higher Education	
State Student Incentive Grants	76,750
Upward Bound	56,000
Talent Search, Post Secondary	15,300
Women's Education Equity	10,000
Educational Opportunity Centers	6,300
Adult Indian Education	5,930
Education, Metric System	1,840
Fulbright-Hays Educational and Cultural Exchange	920
State Student Financial Aid Administration	600
Fulbright-Hays Training Grants, Foreign Study	289
Vocational	
Vocational Education, Special Needs	20,000
Appalachian Vocational and Other Education	19,000
Career Education	10,135
Vocational Education, State Advisory Councils	6,073
Educational TV and Radio	6,000
Vocational Education Improvement Projects	5,236
Community Education	3,138
Bilingual Vocational Training	1,820
Bilingual Vocational Instruction	700
Bilingual Instructional Material, Vocational	280
Research	
Bilingual Education	173,600
Educational Research and Development	98,285
State Educational Agency Needs	50,000
Marine Research, Educational Training	35,236
Handicapped Regional Education Resource Centers	9,750

TABLE C5—Continued

Federal Aid Cluster	FY 1980 Funding
Ethnic Heritage Studies	3,000
Education Information Centers	3,000
Developmental Disabilities, University Affiliated	3,000
Statistical Activities in State Education Agencies	1,550
Foreign Language and Area Studies Research	1,000
13. VOCATIONAL REHABILITATION	
Communicative Disorders Research	29,206
Rehabilitation Research	27,500
Handicapped Research, Education and Demonstration	20,000
Handicapped Research, Early Childhood	20,000
Vision Research, Sensory and Motor	18,718
Rehabilitation Research, Prosthetics	8,005

SOURCE: Advisory Commission on Intergovernmental Regulations.

A Note on the Book

*The typeface used for the text of this book is
Palatino, designed by Hermann Zapf.
The type was set by
FotoTypesetters Incorporated, of Baltimore.
R.R. Donnelley & Sons Company printed
and bound the book, using Warren's Sebago paper.
The cover and format were designed by Pat Taylor,
and the figure drawn by Hördur Karlsson.
The manuscript was edited by S. Ellen Dykes
and by Anne Gurian of the AEI Publications staff.*